RUNNERDOTES
A Collection of Anecdotes from Inspirational Runners

RUNNERDOTES

A Collection of Anecdotes from Inspirational Runners

By
Adrian Mok with The Nutgraf

World Scientific

NEW JERSEY • LONDON • SINGAPORE • BEIJING • SHANGHAI • HONG KONG • TAIPEI • CHENNAI • TOKYO

Published by

World Scientific Publishing Co. Pte. Ltd.
5 Toh Tuck Link, Singapore 596224
USA office: 27 Warren Street, Suite 401-402, Hackensack, NJ 07601
UK office: 57 Shelton Street, Covent Garden, London WC2H 9HE

British Library Cataloguing-in-Publication Data
A catalogue record for this book is available from the British Library.

RUNNERDOTES
A Collection of Anecdotes from Inspirational Runners

Copyright © 2017 by F4U Pte. Ltd. and World Scientific Publishing Co. Pte. Ltd.

All rights reserved. This book, or parts thereof, may not be reproduced in any form or by any means, electronic or mechanical, including photocopying, recording or any information storage and retrieval system now known or to be invented, without written permission from the publisher.

For photocopying of material in this volume, please pay a copying fee through the Copyright Clearance Center, Inc., 222 Rosewood Drive, Danvers, MA 01923, USA. In this case permission to photocopy is not required from the publisher.

ISBN 978-981-3222-12-0 (pbk)

Desk Editor: Jiang Yulin

Designers: Loo Chuan Ming and Kim Joseph Paulo C. Casera

Contents

Conquering the Night 1
Adrian Mok

The Happy Runner 11
Jenny Huang

Keeping the Faith 18
Ashley Liew

Eat, Drink, and Run Merry 26
Lim Baoying

Squeezing It All In 34
Mok Ying Ren

The Experimental Runner 56
Andy Neo

The Road to Rio 66
Neo Jie Shi

Going for Gold 76
Soh Rui Yong

Just Run *86*
Jeanette Wang

From Late Bloomer to SEA Games Athlete *95*
Melvin Wong Yao Hian

Don't Stop Running *102*
Adrian Mok

Conquering the Night

Adrian Mok

Adrian Mok documents the long solo journeys that would eventually lead to the birth of the Sundown Marathon.

For 12 weeks or so in 2005, I embarked on a journey of running an ultramarathon. It was a National Technological University alumni event called Run Round Singapore, and it entailed covering 168 km on a route circumnavigating the entire island of Singapore. While preparing for the event, I started a routine of night running. This journey was to create a meaningful chapter in my life: It would lead to self-discovery, a business, many failures and victories, and significant milestones in life. The training would lead to many moments of ups and downs, allowing me to draw many lessons when I later embarked on the journey of creating the Sundown Marathon.

Runnerdotes

Runnerdotes is a collection of stories dedicated to the Sundown Marathon, which celebrates its 10th edition in 2017. While penning my thoughts, I had observed that in the pursuit of running, there is a universal language that unites most, if not all, runners. We talk about training, nutrition, shoes and all the technical stuff, but what really unites us is our passion, determination and the attitude of never giving up. I believe that our loyal followers — to whom I thank for the evolution of the Sundown Marathon — hold these same values of running.

As I made this discovery, it piqued my interest to delve into the thoughts of the many runners I have met. The people who appear in our first edition of *Runnerdotes* may not be hugely famous. In my opinion, however, they are the ones who have contributed to Singapore's running scene. I met them to talk shop on running and to ask them: What drives you? What pushes you? What picks you up again and makes you go the next mile, the next step? And true enough, as we chatted, I discovered that the language of running is universal. All of us share the core values of passion, resilience and discipline. I dedicate this book to all those who speak this language of love in our pursuit of running.

As with all runs, we take a rest at the pit stops, but we never stop looking forward to the next stop — and to the next run, the next race, and the next challenge. I hope to find more like-minded souls who will be willing to share a tale with me when I pen the next episode of *Runnerdotes*.

11:59 pm, 15 August 2005

When the clock struck 12, it was my moment. My time to repeat my indulgence and masochism. My time to experience the unknown, conquer the fear, deal with the loneliness, and conquer the voice in my head that told me to stop being crazy. There was always apprehension, and yet there was also the longing to embrace every bit of the experience for what it was worth.

I had started building up my endurance slowly, starting from 30 km and proceeding to 40 km and then to 50 km per night. Even though I got stronger and more confident, the solo runs through the night did not get any easier. There was always the tinge of worry and the "what if". What if I get hungry? What if I get tired? What if I run into some kind of trouble? But there was also the voice of positivity that squashed these doubts and told me to just get going.

On this night, my routine proceeded as usual. The movie date night with my wife Jo had been our Friday evening staple when we did not have any kids. Every Friday, we would meet after work and enjoy our romantic ritual at the cinema. Once we headed home, however, Jo would head to bed and I would lace up my running shoes. At this stage of my running career, I already had several marathons and Ironman races under my belt. Still, the long runs never began without some level of anxiety. For a start, there was the question of where to go.

The tiny island of Singapore offers a number of running routes in the north, south, east and west. With late-night running, I was not bounded by traffic or crowds; I simply had to deal with loneliness, the bugbear of all night runs. I could run over any stretch of road, park path, and trail if I wanted to. However, once I had a distance in mind, I had to figure out how I wanted to go about it.

On this night, I decided to take the shortest path from my home in Bukit Batok to East Coast Park via Bukit Timah Road. East Coast Park offered some nice options of late-night food joints and park goers, which made running alone slightly easier to deal with. From my place to Bukit Timah Road was a mere 8 km, but by the time I reached Watten estate, at about 1 am, fatigue had set in.

Runnerdotes

The truth of the matter is that even when you think you have become more seasoned in this routine of running, you will still suffer. But it's a love–hate relationship with suffering. You know there will be moments of great discomfort, so you deal with it by learning to call suffering your friend. On this night, however, I was feeling tired — really tired.

My legs started to feel heavy and my eyelids started to droop. Whatever iron I thought I had possessed, whatever self-motivating pep talk I had given myself — it was all gone this night. So I decided to lie down and rest. I headed towards a small park in the area with the intention of taking a nap. I had taken such power naps frequently during runs; I didn't need to set a time limit, because I could usually get up and get going in about 15 minutes. This time round, however, I crashed into a deep sleep on a park bench.

I awakened to the sound of chanting. The chill of the night told me that it was about 3 am. Kneeling some 10 m from me was a bald, old man of slight built. He was chanting away and bowing repeatedly. I was taken aback — a bit frightened but also annoyed to be awakened from slumber. Not knowing what to make of the situation, I continued to lie on the bench, closing my eyes in an attempt to convince myself that I was done with my meaningless and fruitless run. I was annoyed and disappointed, but I assured myself that I would be back again the next night to redeem myself.

I tried to get back to sleep, but the chanting went on. Then, I felt a weight pressing onto me — just before I saw two soldiers, dressed in old Japanese military uniforms and rifles in their hands, marching past me. This was getting freaky now! I tried to get up but couldn't. Somehow, my mind was fully awake, but I couldn't seem to move my body. This went on till about 4 am, when I finally managed to get out of the long nightmare. Jumping off the bench, I rushed about the park trying to find

Conquering the Night

the frail old man and the two soldiers. They could not be found.

Feeling at a loss and totally unmotivated, I gave up training that night. What began as a run of at least 50 km ended with just 8 km and a strange old man who disrupted my sleep. Was it a hallucination, a figment of my imagination, or an otherworldly experience? Up till today, I have no answers. I walked to the nearest bus stop, still shaken by the experience. There was no more enjoyment to be had in the run, and I took a cab home.

11:59 pm, 5 September 2005

Ever since the spooky encounter, I had found a new strategy: Find friends to accompany me on certain stretches of the crazy journeys. I was indeed blessed to have a couple of friends who subscribed to my nonsensical request. Every week, I would find a new route to keep me excited and looking forward to the run, find friends who lived along the route, and arrange to meet them at a designated time.

On this night, the main course on the menu started with Bukit Batok and Bukit Timah Road, headed north along Mandai Road to Seletar, then to Punggol, almost reaching Pasir Ris, before turning into East Coast Park and finishing in the city for breakfast. In essence, it was a clockwise circumnavigation of Singapore, from the west to the north to the east and finally to the south. The choice of friend for that day was a dear friend, now Minister of State Teo Ser Luck.

The usual midnight routine resumed. As Friday turned into Saturday, I set out on my journey. This route was by far my longest, taking in parts that I had not ventured during the night before. As I passed the Mandai Hill Camp along Mandai Road, I spotted two dogs lying near the camp gate. Sensing danger, I quickly crossed over to the other side of the road, hoping that I would not arouse their curiosity. Luck was not quite

 *Runnerdotes*

on my side; as feared, they stood up, stared momentarily at me — and gave chase. Not quite the dog whisperer, I decided that I did not stand any chance against them.

So I sprinted. I sprinted like I had never sprinted before. In that one single effort, I'm sure I broke my 200-m personal best. I'm sure I could feel dog breath on my calves. I swore that I would never complain again about doing my interval sets and say that they would not help in my marathon pursuit. And I swore never to run alone at night again.

The two dogs slowed down after about 200 m, but continued trailing behind me, never quite giving up their pursuit. I slowed down to catch my breath too, looking behind me from time to time. But the two dogs sped up again. Cursing — even though I was out of breath — I broke into my second sprint. I ran onto the road in a zig-zag, hoping for oncoming traffic to kill the dogs. When that didn't happen, I braced myself to battle them with my bare fists.

Thank goodness, the four-legged "friends" were not the best in the endurance game, and gave up eventually. But the drama had given me an adrenaline rush, better than any caffeine shot. I continued the run, my elevated heart rate matching the beat of my music.

At Seletar, I met Ser Luck, and we decided to take a shortcut to East Coast Park through an industrial area instead of a long detour through Pasir Ris. There, I heard dogs barking again. This time, however, courage prevailed with the knowledge that I had a two-legged friend with me. We slowed to a walk to appear less aggressive as we left their territory, and the dogs did not give chase. It was just as well — I doubt I could survive another chase.

Our journey continued in peace as we bypassed Bedok and reached East Coast Park via Changi. By that time, it was past 6.30 am. The horizon was lit up by the rising sun in an almost purplish hue, a breathtaking sight. But the wind was also picking up, signalling an approaching storm, and within 30 minutes, the sun was consumed entirely by a heavy thunderstorm. It was like seeing a time-lapse video; the rapid transition from sunrise to thunderstorm was a metaphor for life, of times of joy and periods of hardship. If there was a moment of epiphany and inspiration for the Sundown Marathon, I think this was it.

We were not prepared for the storm. Happily aborting the run, we had the perfect excuse to stop for a warm breakfast. It was a dramatic end to a long, eventful night — and the beginning of something big.

> Running a race is never about crossing the finish line. The moment of relief comes in crossing the line, but true joy comes from relishing how you reached that line; how hard you worked to get there.
> Be it a victory scream or sheer disappointment when you crossed the line, this is the moment of reflection.
> One that defines how you desire to do it better again despite repeatedly putting yourself to the grind during training.
> It is always about the journey and not just the destination.

Adrian Mok

The Happy Runner

Jenny Huang
Sundown Ultra Marathon 2013 — Women's champion

It all started with the uncles.

Jenny Huang had wanted to lose some weight after her second pregnancy, and was also struggling with some personal issues. A bit of running, she thought, would help cut her weight and also relieve her stress. So she went down to a park connector in Ghim Moh that was popular with joggers, and started down the path. And that's when she saw the uncles.

They looked to be in their 50s and even 60s, had grey hair, and did not sport the latest running fashions. Some even had paunches. Yet they ran at an impressive pace that left many younger runners behind — including Jenny.

"All the uncles were faster than me!" exclaims the bubbly 44-year-old.

Runnerdotes

The naturally competitive mother of two couldn't bear to be beaten, so she went back to the park connector regularly, running for 10 minutes at a time, then 15 minutes. "I said, 'I will beat one of these uncles one day.' And one day, I finally beat one, and he clapped for me! And I was really happy."

The mini-achievement sparked a love for running. Up till then, Jenny's only exposure to the sport was "running from dogs" when she grew up in Texas. Born in Taiwan, her family had moved to the United States, where she spent much of her childhood outdoors. "I was never a runner in school," she says. "I just played outside a lot, got chased by dogs a lot. As a kid. I ran around a lot, so I was fairly fit."

But she didn't start running proper until 2007, after she moved to Singapore to work. Her daughter Zoe, then six, was attending primary school and son Austin, three, had started preschool, giving her some free time. Her little victory over the Ghim Moh uncles encouraged her to go farther and longer, and then to sign up for a 10 km race. To her own surprise, she did well and even found that she still had "a lot of energy left". So she did what seemed natural to her — set her sights on a marathon, because "that's what people were doing".

In 2009, she ran her first marathon, crossing the finish line in just under four hours. This easily put her in the top 10 percent — a very creditable time indeed for a first-time marathoner.

By then, she had discovered how fun and therapeutic running could be — and how good she was. The self-confessed "endorphin junkie" says: "When I first started, it was for fun, to stay fit. Then when I started winning some small obscure races, I was like, I think I'm pretty decent!"

Her successes prompted her to join a track team, which saw her doing intervals, tempo runs and long runs. While family and work commitments eventually made it difficult to keep up, it showed her the value of structured training, which she continued under her fiancé Steven Chan, a running and swimming coach.

It was Steven who in 2013 gave Jenny the idea of something she had never considered: The Sundown Ultramarathon, which would push her well beyond the usual 42.195 km she was doing. Covering 100 km, it was the equivalent of almost 2½ marathons.

The decision to take on the challenge turned out to be a journey Jenny would never forget. Apart from the seven or eight long months of intensive training it would entail — including daily 20 km runs — it was also a time of personal emotional therapy: Soon after she signed up, her father was diagnosed with fourth-stage liver cancer.

"He was fighting it really hard, and he passed away four months after diagnosis," she recalls. "The training time gave me time to cry, to find strength through my dad, and to find strength in myself."

After her father passed away, she drew strength from a determination to honour his memory and his never-give-up attitude to life. This sustained her through the ultramarathon, which she describes as "ultra painful".

The first 50 km, she says, was easy enough. But the second half was tough. "When I hit the 84 km mark, I thought, 'I just did two marathons! I can stop now!' But I couldn't. I pushed hard and kept telling myself not to stop, not to walk. I just kept saying to myself, 'Jenny, Jenny, keep going'." In between, Jenny, who is a Christian, also spent time during the race "chatting" with her dad.

She also pays tribute to the two support cyclists who kept her company through the night. "One of them nearly fell asleep and nearly fell off his bike," she recalls. "But he really helped me. He kept saying, 'C'mon, girl, you're almost home'."

In the end, she not only finished the race strong, but also beat every

 *Runnerdotes*

other female competitor, crossing the line with an impressive timing of 10 hrs 38 mins 9 secs — more than one hour ahead of the next woman.

That Sundown Ultramarathon, she says without hesitation, was her most memorable race of her life. "That race was very significant for me, it was the way God planned it," she says. "It was an amazing experience."

Amazing performance, however, is not the most striking thing you'll discover about Jenny; it's how happy she is as a runner. Talk to her about running, and you'll find her cracking jokes about herself and laughing nonstop, and talking about how *wonderful* running is.

"I don't like negativity," she explains. A positive attitude was what helped her through the most difficult times in her life, and she has not forgotten that lesson. "When you hit rock-bottom, the only place you're going is up. So ever since then I've only ever gone up. It doesn't do any good to be negative."

Running, she adds, has given her "soul". "I love the 'me' time. I love running alone. I love listening to music."

She also loves pushing herself, and is more than happy to wake up long before the sun rises each morning to throw in the miles so that she is done by 8 am. Long distance races, she knows, require nothing less than hard work — putting in the mileage and continually pushing one's endurance farther and farther.

"I love the rush from being pushed too much," she says unabashedly. "Most runners are extremists. We like that rush, we love being fit, we love pushing our body to the extent that we ask ourselves, 'Is this pain or is this just me being tired?' At the end of the day, it's not about my timing; I am truly happy when I know I gave my 110 percent before any race. I find a lot of happiness in knowing that I am still able to push that. It's mental, totally mental."

Despite all the talk about pushing herself, however, she knows where to draw the line. Even though she may love the long runs, she doesn't compromise on rest and recovery. As a full-time physiotherapist, she knows better. Ask her about injuries, and she gets serious.

"If I'm truly injured, I do take off from training. I don't like missing training days, but I will have one rest day, because it's important for recovery," she says. She also makes full use of various techniques and technology to reduce the risk of injury, such as stretching, strengthening exercises for specific parts of the body, rotating between different shoes, cross-training, trail running, and taping — applying elastic tape to support and stabilise parts of the legs.

"I see a lot of cases of knee pain and plantar fascia," she says. "Research has shown that main source of knee pain is lack of hip extension — the range of motion. When we sit a lot, we lose a lot of range, so we need to strengthen the butt."

So she makes sure she does her hill runs, exercises to strengthen the gluteal muscles, and foam rolling to loosen tight muscles. She also keeps a healthy diet that includes simple carbohydrates, lots of liquids, and enough rest before and after long runs.

Of course, she never lets all these considerations take away from the simple joys of running.

"Running has taught me to follow my passion," she says. "It's taught me to calm down a lot and think things through. As a physiotherapist, I get a lot of things from running. I can understand my clients who are athletic, as well as the ones who are not, to inspire them. You can't tell someone to exercise if you yourself are not doing it."

> " I love the rush from being pushed too much. Most runners are extremists. We like that rush, we love being fit, we love pushing our body to the extent that we ask ourselves, 'Is this pain or is this just me being tired?' At the end of the day, it's not about my timing; I am truly happy when I know I gave my 110 percent before any race. I find a lot of happiness in knowing that I am still able to push that. It's mental, totally mental. "

Jenny Huang

Keeping the Faith

Ashley Liew

The first time Ashley Liew and his coach Rameshon met, the trainer had only one thing to say. Pointing to his new student's tummy, the former running champion said, "This still needs to go down."

"That," recalls Ashley, "was the first sentence he said to me."

It is hard to imagine that this same young man who once tipped the scales at 80 kg would one day represent Singapore in a marathon at the South-east Asian Games. But, as the now-57 kg top runner notes with much gratitude, he had a coach who believed in him. "He saw some hidden potential in me that even I didn't recognise," he says. "I'm really glad that he saw that."

You could call Ashley an accidental runner — or an inspired one. He was first moved to start running for a simple reason: To lose weight.

"When you grow up overweight in school, you get teased a lot. And

I got teased quite a bunch. Some nicknames really stuck," he says. "It affected my self-esteem and my self-confidence."

Looking for a way to channel his frustration and to "find my self-worth", he turned to running. "It was purely by chance," he says.

So was his entrance to the world of marathons and long-distance running. On a whim, he and some schoolmates signed up for the Singapore Marathon in 2004, while they were still in junior college. Ashley found himself struggling to finish it in 4 hrs 29 mins 34 secs. "When you're carrying all that weight for a marathon, you feel it," he says. "I was at the back of the pack and really struggling. But I liked the idea of pushing myself."

That debut saw him run a marathon every year from then on — although, as the ever-humble runner notes, his progress was "very incremental, very slow". So slow, he stresses, that he did not even make the reserve team for the officer cadets' Army Half Marathon squad in 2005 while he was serving national service.

Still, the progress he saw in his dropping weight encouraged him to keep plodding on — and even to try out triathlons. By now, he was beginning to enjoy running for its own sake, and he soon found a joy in the multi-sport races too. "I really enjoyed the feeling of racing, switching from the swim to the bike, and then to the run. Running was my much stronger suit, so it was nice to play catch up on the run," he says.

Eventually, he would complete two Ironman triathlons, clocking a personal best (PB) of 10 hrs 3 mins 29 secs, and two Ironman 70.3 World Championships.

But the biggest turnaround in his running came in December 2008, when he came under the tutelage of Rameshon, who holds Singapore's national marathon record of 2 hrs 24 mins 22 secs. That came about when the track and field club and aquathlon club at the Singapore Management

 *Runnerdotes*

University, where Ashley was studying, engaged the veteran runner as a long-distance running coach.

By then, Ashley had brought his marathon timing down to 3 hrs 34 mins 14 secs. Within a year, however, Rameshon helped him cut it down to 2 hrs 51 mins 22 secs. This timing gave him a second place in the local men's category in the Singapore Marathon — and turned a "nobody" in the sports scene into a local potential.

"I had a lot of people tell me that it was impossible, it was not conventional wisdom," he says. "I'm glad I didn't listen to conventional wisdom. I had a coach who believed in me."

The remarkable improvement gave Ashley a newfound confidence that he could cut his time even further — which he did. In 2011, he clocked his personal best at the Gold Coast Marathon, finishing at 2 hrs 41 mins 55 secs, and the following year, came in tops in the local men's category of the Singapore Marathon.

In 2015, he would push his PB down even further, clocking 2 hrs 32 mins 12 secs at the New Orleans Rock 'n' Roll Marathon while placing overall runner-up among an international field.

"It comes with confidence," he says of the breakthrough. "The faster time you clock, the more confident you get and the more you believe it's possible."

"It's a lot of self-belief and also having people like Coach Rameshon instilling self-confidence in me. It's something I need to continue working on and keep believing in. You have to keep the faith."

That faith kept him going and helped him qualify for the SEA Games in 2013 and again in 2015. It was at the second Games in Singapore, however, that he really made his mark — not by winning, ironically, but by losing. Deliberately.

When the lead runners in the marathon missed a turn early on in the race, Ashley, who was at the back of the pack, suddenly found himself at the front. This gave him an advantage and a chance of getting a podium position — and a much-coveted medal — but he decided to slow down to allow the others to catch up. He eventually finished eighth. Asked why he made that fateful decision, he replied he valued sportsmanship above all, and just could not see himself taking advantage of the situation.

The move was widely praised, and he made the headlines the next day. Soon after, he made it into the news again when he become the first Singaporean to be awarded the Pierre de Coubertin World Fair Play Trophy in the "Act of Fair Play" category. The ceremony was held in Budapest, Hungary.

Ask Ashley what is his secret to his success, and the soft-spoken runner is quick to credit Rameshon. "Coach keeps a watchful eye on my training, catching wrong techniques before they become a bad habit," he says. "That has played a huge role. I also take my rest seriously — when it's time to rest, I really try to rest."

He learnt this lesson from watching top-notch Kenyan runners, he says. "A good reason why they do so well is that they really do nothing in between their morning and evening training sessions," he observes. "They take naps; they have a lot of time to focus on running. Their level of dedication is unparalleled."

Ashley tries to juggle his 160 km-a-week routine and his work as a Doctor of Chiropractic. Fortunately, he says, his hours at the Family Health Chiropractic Clinic where he works are fixed, giving him time to squeeze in an early morning run before work, and an evening run after knocking off.

"Running for me is like brushing your teeth in the morning," he says simply. "It's just something I'll do whether I'm tired or not. Just keep the consistency on a day-to-day basis, keep that belief in yourself, and

Runnerdotes

hopefully things will fall into place."

But he also tries to keep to a disciplined routine. When he is done at the clinic, he heads straight to the track or gym for training, then home for dinner. "If I need to catch up with anything on the computer or with friends, I might do that, but most of the time I will go straight home for dinner and then straight to rest," he says. "You have to keep a consistent pattern."

He remains adamant that he will not give up his practice for running, nor the other way round. Besides, he adds, chiropractic — which allows for restoration of the body's optimum musculoskeletal system potential through the nervous system — has helped him avoid injuries. He has not suffered a single training injury since 2010, when he first started receiving chiropractic care.

"Chiropractic deals with the alignment of the whole system — not just the bones, but the whole nervous system," he explains. "The nervous system controls everything, so it needs to be balanced."

On race day, he also keeps to a simple routine. He gets up early so that he has time for breakfast to digest, as well as for some warming up and stretching at home. This ensures that he doesn't have to worry about fighting for space to stretch at the race site.

He also spends time preparing for the race mentally, visualising it and — uniquely — keeping calm. While some runners would play fast music to pep themselves up, he does the opposite. "I play calm music because you don't want to be too amped up before running," he says.

During the race, he keeps it just as simple. By his own admission, he does not think too much as he is running. "I'm focused on the present moment — what's happening at that exact time," he explains. "I'm not too caught up in the past or worried about the future. Maybe I'll look at my immediate environment to make sure I'm taking the right turns and check my pace and running form. And if I'm having a rough patch, I say a mantra, like 'strength and grace, strength and grace', to reinforce my self-belief."

Indeed, he is a big believer in positive thinking. You always have to keep the faith and believe in yourself, he says — just as the once-pudgy teen did when he signed up for his first marathon.

Today, he is setting his sights on the next Olympics in 2020. "I just need to believe in myself," he says. "And I will prioritise work and training where needed. There is a time to prioritise work, and a time to prioritise training. These go hand in hand."

> "Running for me is like brushing your teeth in the morning. It's just something I'll do whether I'm tired or not. Just keep the consistency on a day-to-day basis, keep that belief in yourself, and hopefully things will fall into place."

Ashley Liew

Eat, Drink, and Run Merry

Lim Baoying
Sundown Marathon 2010 — Women's Open champion
Sundown Marathon 2011 — Women's Open 4th
Sundown Half Marathon 2012 — Women's Open 2nd
Sundown Marathon 2013 — Women's Open 5th
Sundown Ultra Marathon 2015 — Team of 4 relay Mixed 1st

As a sports doctor, Lim Baoying is used to patients coming in with three common injuries: Runner's Knee (Patellofemoral pain syndrome), Runner's Heel (Plantar fasciitis), and shin splints (medial tibial stress syndrome).

Not surprisingly, most of these conditions are the result of running. With more and more Singaporeans taking part in races — especially those of longer distances, like marathons — related injuries are on the rise.

But Baoying is quick to make one thing clear: Running doesn't cause injuries.

"It is the way you run that causes injury," says the 35-year-old. "Some people start off too much, too fast, and don't allow their bodies to rest enough. That's one of the top reasons for injury. Because there are so many races in Singapore and our weather allows year-round training, most of us do not practise any form of rest. The accumulation of mileage is a recipe for injury."

She also advises getting the right shoes — and avoiding the wrong ones. "Don't hesitate to throw away a pair of shoes when it causes you pain, symptoms or some injury that doesn't go away," she stresses. "A pair of shoes can make or break your run."

Different makes and models, she notes, place stresses on different body parts. Runners need to experiment and find out which ones suit their body shape and size and running styles, as well as where they run and how far. This could mean trying out different brands and models, if budget permits. What about the recent trend of barefoot running? Baoying goes back to the main principle: As long as it works for you and it causes no injury, go ahead and try it out.

But she is more insistent on things like nutrition and hydration. She has found that not eating and drinking adequately can affect her performance, especially for longer runs. While one could pop out for a short run of say, 30 minutes or less, without worrying about food or water, longer ones will need more careful planning. This means making sure one can get water along the way, or having a proper dinner with the right mixture of carbohydrates and protein the night before. That, she says, puts "fuel in your tank".

Marathons require even more advance planning. She recommends increasing caloric intake (commonly referred to as "carbo-loading") up to one week before the race to improve the body's storage of glycogen. Combined with reduced mileage in the period of tapering, this may result in a bit of bloatedness. But, she adds: "Your body will thank you when you're running the 42 km."

The careful planning extends right into the race itself. As a

marathon typically takes an average runner five or six hours, the body needs constant top-ups of fuel and liquids. Baoying suggests taking an energy gel after the first hour, and one every 45 minutes or so after that, along with electrolyte drinks at the water stations.

But while runners are likely to keep a close watch on their diets, she opts for a more moderate approach. "If you're training regularly for long distance, sometimes you just need to give in to your indulgences," she says. "You need to treat your body better so that you can be a better athlete and not be a grumpy athlete because of too many food restrictions."

All this advice, however, doesn't come from a textbook or training manual. It comes from years of personal experience. The senior staff registrar at Changi Sports Medicine Centre is an accomplished swimmer, cyclist and runner who has done many marathons, duathlons, triathlons, and other endurance events, and has notched up a number of notable victories.

These include winning the Women's Open category in the Sundown Marathon 2010, taking the podium in many local races, and representing Singapore at the Ironman 70.3 World Championships 2015.

Not bad, indeed, for a once-overweight girl who was the slowest runner in her class in primary school. "I couldn't stand being the slowest in class any more, so in secondary school, I started running on my own. Before school started, I would go and run around the school compound," she recalls.

It was probably there that her love for running began. In secondary school, she became a physical training instructor in the National Police Cadet Corps, which gave her further incentive to be fit, so as to be an example to younger cadets. When she went on to junior college, she thought of going into sprinting, but was referred to the distance coach instead. Since then, she has not looked back.

Eat, Drink, and Run Merry

Needless to say, Baoying is a strong proponent of running. Anyone, she says, can run. "It is a non-technical sport anyone can get into," she says. "You put your left foot in front, your right foot stays behind. Then your right foot goes in front, leaving your left foot behind. Your arms go in the opposite direction. How easy can any sports be? You can't go very wrong."

Running, she adds, is also one of the cheapest sports — all a newbie needs is a pair of shoes, socks, top, shorts, "and off you go".

Ask her why anyone should run, and she is quick to give a long list of reasons. Running allows you to connect with yourself. Whether you run alone or with friends, you are likely to be in your own world, focusing on the rhythm of your breathing, hearing each footfall, and taking in the fresh air. Running gives you relief from stress, and like any other sports, releases endorphins that make you feel good about yourself. "So why not? Everyone should get into this sport called running."

She has her own memorable experience of the joy of running. Ironically, she discovered it because of her competitiveness. "I say I'm chill, but deep inside I can't stand it if I put in a lousy run and don't perform to my own standards," she admits.

So, at one marathon, feeling that she was not up to scratch, she removed the timing chip from her running bib and threw it away before she began. The timing chip, a small device attached to the bib, allows race organisers to track a runner as he or she crosses the finish line, and gives an official record of the runner's timing. She figured that she would rather complete the run without an official timing, than have black-and-white proof of what she felt would be a poor timing.

Incredibly, she ended up doing a PB — a Personal Best, or the best timing she had ever done. Her running buddy, who was keeping pace alongside, had timed the run and told her. "If I had retained my chip,

 *Runnerdotes*

I would have been ranked within the top 10 female finishers," she says ruefully. "I regretted it. But I can't take back what I did."

But she made another even more valuable discovery. "I was able to smile for the whole time during the race," she recalls. "When I subsequently saw the race photos, they showed me smiling."

What she found was that running without a timing chip — and thus without the stress of doing well — took a big burden off her shoulders. That marathon taught her not to take things too seriously, and also not to doubt herself. After all, she says, "it's just a run".

The avid runner has also learnt to run her own race, and not to worry about what people think of her performance. She urges runners to shrug off others' expectations or unhelpful opinions. "Do they know what's going on in your life — what you are dealing with, what you are training for, or if there is anything else affecting you?" she points out. "No one can answer those questions except yourself. Life is short anyway. It's just a run. It's not a do-or-die issue every time you run."

Every runner, she says, just needs to answer to himself or herself. Put in a decent effort, she advises, and don't beat yourself over the head if you don't do well.

"Numbers can kill the enjoyment. Running is supposed to help you connect with yourself, your whole psyche, and make you feel good about yourself. So if all these things crowd your experience, then why run?"

Eat, Drink, and Run Merry

Baoying's Running Tips

Mileage:
Don't start off running too much or too fast.

Allow your body to get enough rest in between runs and races.

Shoes:
Don't keep wearing shoes that cause you pain or injuries.

Get the right shoe.

If you can, experiment with different shoes and find out which ones suit your weight and running style, and the distance and terrain you usually run.

Hydration/nutrition:
Plan your nutrition for longer runs, such as having a proper dinner the night before. In marathons, eat more calories in the right proportions in the week leading up to the race.

During a long run like a marathon, stay hydrated and fuelled, such as having regular intake of energy gels and electrolyte drinks.

Picture moment with fellow comrades Neo Jieshi and Rachel See at the start line of Great Eastern Women Road 2015.

Hammering it out at the Pocari Sweat Run 2016.

Holding great form at the YOLO Run 2016. (photo credit: Shaun Ho)

" Running is a non-technical sport anyone can get into. You put your left foot in front, your right foot stays behind. Then your right foot goes in front, leaving your left foot behind. Your arms go in the opposite direction. How easy can any sports be? You can't go very wrong. "

Lim Baoying

Squeezing It All In

Mok Ying Ren

Mok Ying Ren does not do things by halves. A casual weekend run in the park, a lazy swim in the pool, or an easy university course just would not have cut it for him. At just 29, he has already squeezed numerous achievements into his lanky frame.

Top cross-country runner in secondary school. Top triathlete in junior college. Medical doctor. South-east East Asian Games gold medallist for triathlon. SEA Games medallist for marathon. National record holder for the half-marathon and 5,000 m.

Most people would have difficulty achieving one or two items in this list, but Ying Ren has managed to do it all before hitting 30. Indeed, one of his hallmarks is his ability to balance studies, work and sports. His secret? Learning to make every minute, hour and day of his life count.

When his medical studies started demanding more of his time, for example, he decided to focus on running, even though he had great potential as a triathlete, having won a gold medal in the sport at the SEA Games in 2007.

"Running was the more time-efficient sport that I could handle," he reveals. "Training involved running from my doorstep and back. There was no time wasted, unlike having to travel to the pool. I liked the whole efficiency of it."

Then, after he graduated and had to shuttle between various hospitals and clinics as a trainee doctor, he made the most of his time by running home — in Tampines — from work, which could be far as Khoo Teck Puat Hospital in Yishun. "I appreciated how I could easily squeeze my work clothes and shoes into a running backpack and begin the commute through the extensive network of park connectors," he says.

It is hard to imagine that he became a runner almost by accident, but that is exactly what happened. In primary school, he was a better swimmer than he was a runner. But in secondary school, along with everyone else, he had to take part in an annual cross-country race around MacRitchie Reservoir. That was when he discovered his natural talent. "I think I came in top 10 in that event in my first year of secondary school, and that piqued my interest in long distance running," he says.

Quickly pulled into the Raffles Institution's cross-country team, he came in 11th in the annual inter-school championships. "My first inter-school race took place after a heavy downpour and it was challenging dealing with the race conditions. I remember vividly how during that race, a fellow runner ended up falling into the reservoir," he recalls. "The rain had caused the water level of the reservoir to rise close to the puddles at one point along the course and he had stepped into it unwittingly. Long-distance running may not be the most glamorous sport, but it definitely has its moments of excitement!"

At the same time, Ying Ren was still training in the pool — and

Runnerdotes

excelling at it. In junior college, he combined his dual interests in running and swimming with cycling, and started representing Singapore in regional triathlon races, eventually winning a gold medal at the SEA Games in 2007.

Upon entering medical school, however, he decided to focus solely on running instead, as he was better able to keep up with training and studying at the same time. His hard work saw him racking up victories in local and regional races, including a win in the local men's category in his debut at the Singapore Marathon in 2009. It was a position he would hold for three consecutive years — all achieved while pursuing his medical studies. He eventually went on to win the title for a record seven times. In 2011, he clocked personal bests of 2 hrs 26 mins 34 secs at the Christchurch Marathon in New Zealand, and 1 hr 8 mins 18 secs at the Bareno Run half-marathon — a national record — in Kuala Lumpur, Malaysia.

It was in 2013, however, that he faced the biggest challenge of balancing work, studies and sports. He had been selected to represent Singapore in the marathon at the SEA Games in December, but still had to fulfil his duties as a House Officer — and also prepare for his enlistment into national service in the same month.

"It was really difficult juggling running training with my long and unpredictable working hours," he recalls. "I had to manage my time very carefully just to continue running twice a day — a short 30-minute run in the morning and a longer run in the evenings."

Around October, he had a month's break before his enlistment. Most people would have taken the opportunity to rest and relax a little after six years of intense studying and clinical attachments to qualify as a professional doctor — but not Ying Ren. He headed to Japan for a one-month training camp, where he joined local runners in putting in

200 km-weeks and even clocked a national record 1 hr 7 mins 53 secs at the Ageo City Half Marathon.

Coming back to Singapore, he ran the Singapore Marathon as part of his heat acclimatisation plan, just a day before enlisting for the Medical Officer Cadet Course, a three-month affair which saw him running around camp with field packs and doing route marches. The exertion strained his hip muscles and gave him a dry cough, which did not recover until he headed to Myanmar for the SEA Games. "I was still on cough syrup a day before the race," he recalls.

In typical fashion, the marathon runner managed to do everything all at once. A day before the race, having just came home from camp the previous night, Ying Ren flew to Myanmar, took a drive of several hours to the Games Village, and had a quick driving tour of the marathon route. Less than 24 hours later, he was at the start line, lined up alongside formidable competitors from across the region. Despite the hectic schedule and his recent recovery from his cough, he managed to clock a time of 2 hrs 28 mins 35 secs — clinching Singapore's first gold in the event since 1983.

"My preparation wasn't optimal," he says, "but I was glad to still come back with a gold medal."

Reflecting on his two SEA Games victories, he adds, "Both times I was up against more experienced, professional athletes while neck-deep in medical school and outfield training. Sometimes, I feel that I do better when the odds are against me, as it forces me to put in 100 percent determination and attention."

The 2013 SEA Games marathon victory also gave him the confidence to aim for something bigger: the Rio Olympics in 2016. But first, he had to bring down his marathon timing to 2 hrs 19 mins to qualify.

"I genuinely felt it was achievable as I had three years to cut 7 mins

 *Runnerdotes*

off my best time of 2 hrs 26 mins," he says. "I felt that if I could commit to my training, including taking one year off work to train full-time, it would be possible."

In the meantime, he set his sights on shorter-term goals, such as taking part in the Commonwealth Games in 2014 and defending his title at the next SEA Games in 2015.

Unfortunately, the intensified training took a toll on his body. He was hit by shin splints, which ultimately took him out of both races. He only managed to regain his momentum at the end of 2014.

In January 2016, he ran a time of 1 hr 7 mins 8 secs half-marathon in Arizona — a new half-marathon national record and a PB. In May, he decided to take part in the Ottawa Marathon in Canada, hoping to get his Olympic qualification there. "But luck was not on my side," he laments. "Despite it being traditionally known as a cool-weather marathon, on the day of the race, it so happened to be the hottest day that Ottawa had experienced in the last 30 years. The race was almost called off."

Still, he managed to run a "respectable" 2 hrs 27 mins. While the missed opportunity to take part in the Rio Olympics hurt, it proved to be an important lesson for him. And that was: Go slow. Over the years, the runner has learnt the value of patience and holding back, especially in training.

When he was suffering from shin splints, he had tried to handle them with "as much common sense as possible". "But the runner in me was impatient," he says. "It was easy to advise patients but hard to heed my own advice! Sometimes, I could not get myself to stop training for a while to allow the injury to heal. Instead, I continued pushing. This led to the injury getting worse."

Most of his injuries, he says, came from over-intensive training. "I used to run up Mount Faber for 10 sets. This session would easily take up to an hour and put me at risk of injury. It would have been wiser to train with moderation and focus on consistency and the long-term."

He was reminded of this lesson again when he came under the tutelage of Lee Troop, a former Australian Olympian and the head coach of Boulder Track Club in Colorado, where Ying Ren spent 12 months training while on no-pay leave in 2016.

Lee taught the Singaporean to tune down his training and take the K.I.S.S. approach to running — Keep It Simple, Stupid. This entailed keeping to the same training schedule, week after week, with the ultimate goal of doing the same for months and years. Says Ying Ren: "It was interesting that the workouts we did there were lower in volume than what I did in Singapore, allowing me to recover better between workouts. It probably reduced my injury risk."

He admits, however, that it took time to adapt to this new approach. "It was not easy to change the mindset as I felt I was doing too little. I tended to do my easy runs too hard or too long."

At Boulder, he also learnt about patience. "It took time to gain confidence in the training programme and fully put my trust into it," he lets on. "Several of the runners I trained with achieved breakthroughs in their racing after being in the same training programme for years. A year may be too short to tell if a training programme works. I realised that there is really no short cut in running."

This patience and level-headedness is serving him well today. Having begun his orthopaedic surgery residency, he is comfortable with having to spend more time on doctoring and less on running — which he works into his schedule by running home on work days.

"I have for most of my life been a 'part-time' athlete and I think I will do just fine," he says. "It is important to re-adjust the expectations that I put on myself to avoid getting burnouts and unnecessary stress."

> " It took time to gain confidence in the training programme and fully put my trust into it. Several of the runners I trained with achieved breakthroughs in their racing after being in the same training programme for years. A year may be too short to tell if a training programme works. I realised that there is really no short cut in running. I have for most of my life been a 'part-time' athlete and I think I will do just fine. It is important to re-adjust the expectations that I put on myself to avoid getting burnouts and unnecessary stress. "

Mok Ying Ren

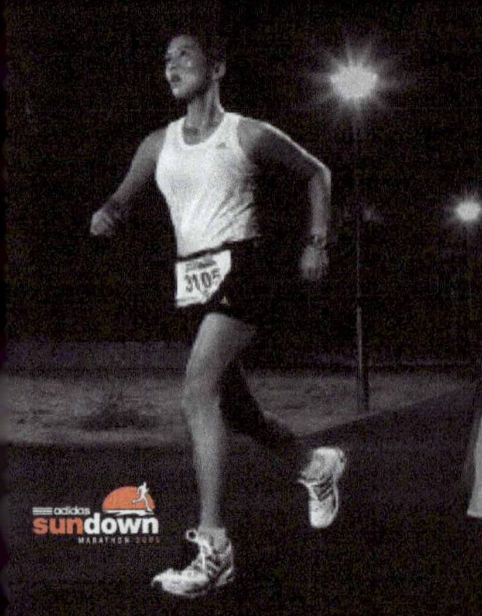
adidas
sundown

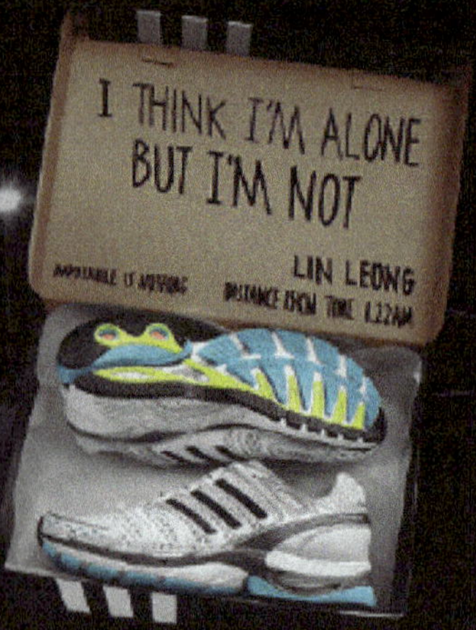
I THINK I'M ALONE
BUT I'M NOT
LIN LEONG

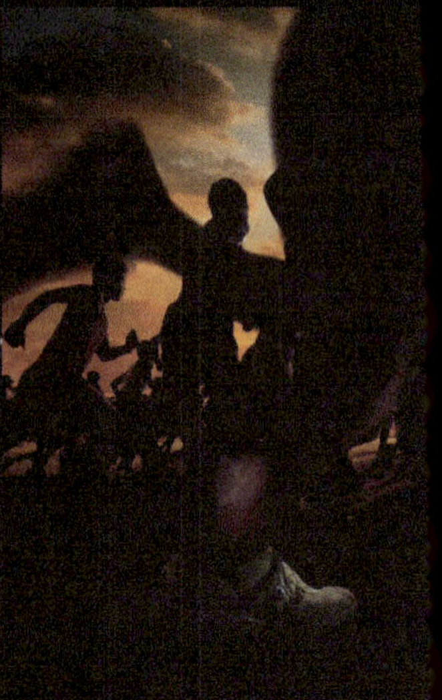

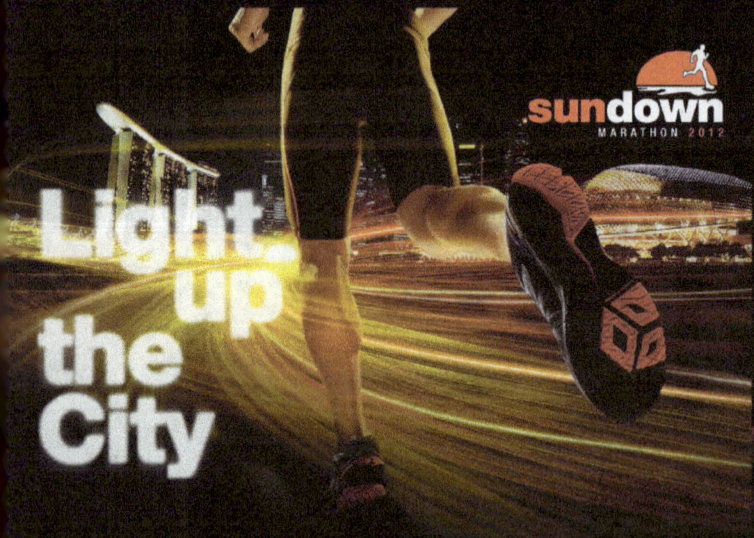
sundown
MARATHON 2012
Light up the City

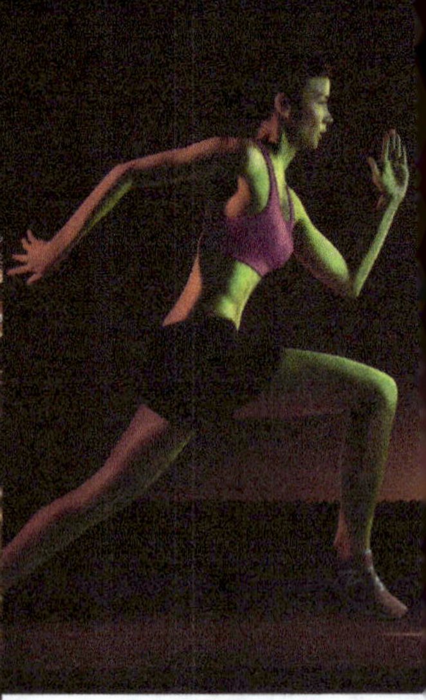

OSIM
sundown
PULSE OF THE
TRIBE
sundown

LIMI

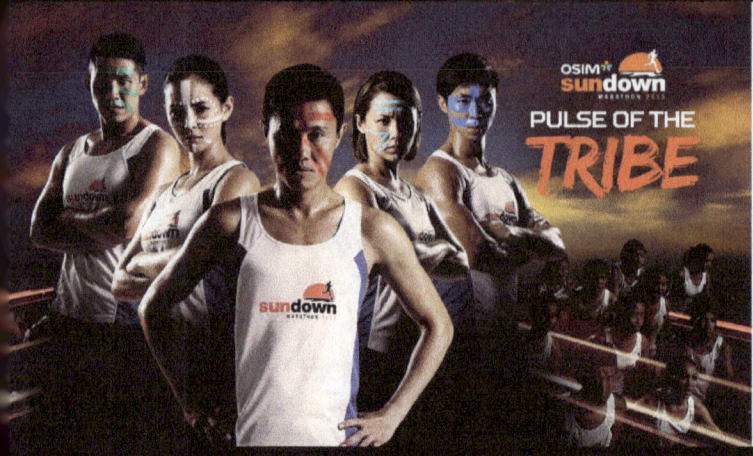

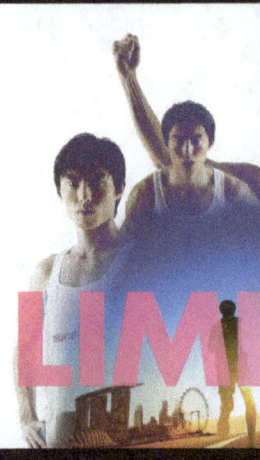

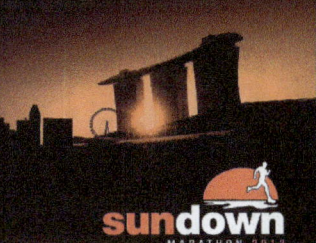

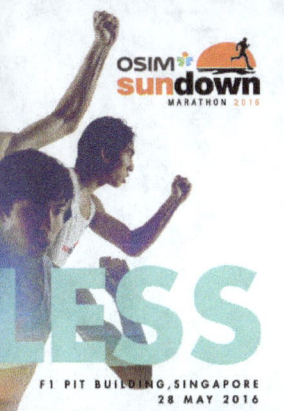

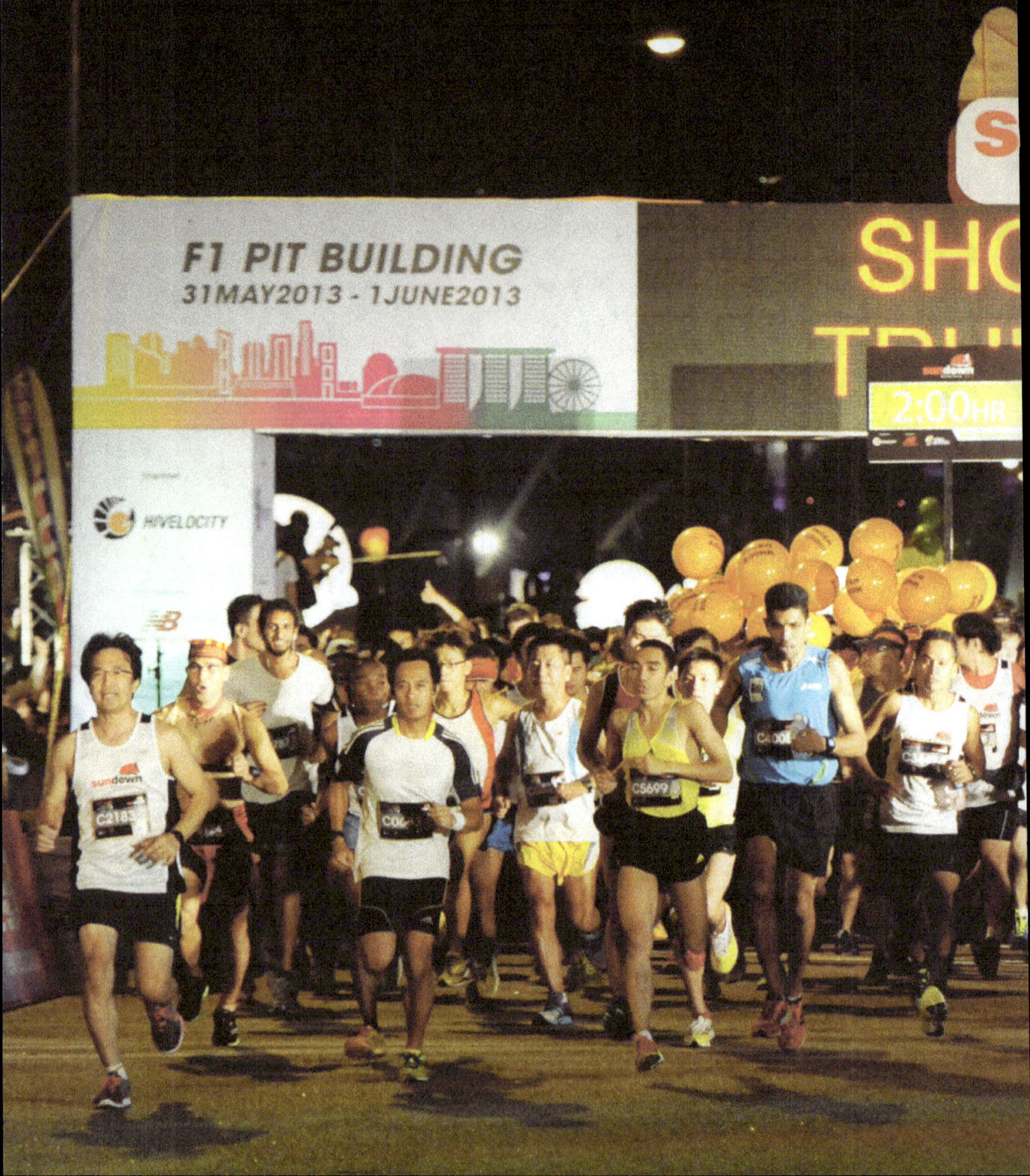
F1 PIT BUILDING
31MAY2013 - 1JUNE2013
HIVELOCITY
2:00HR

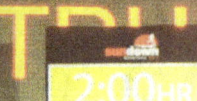

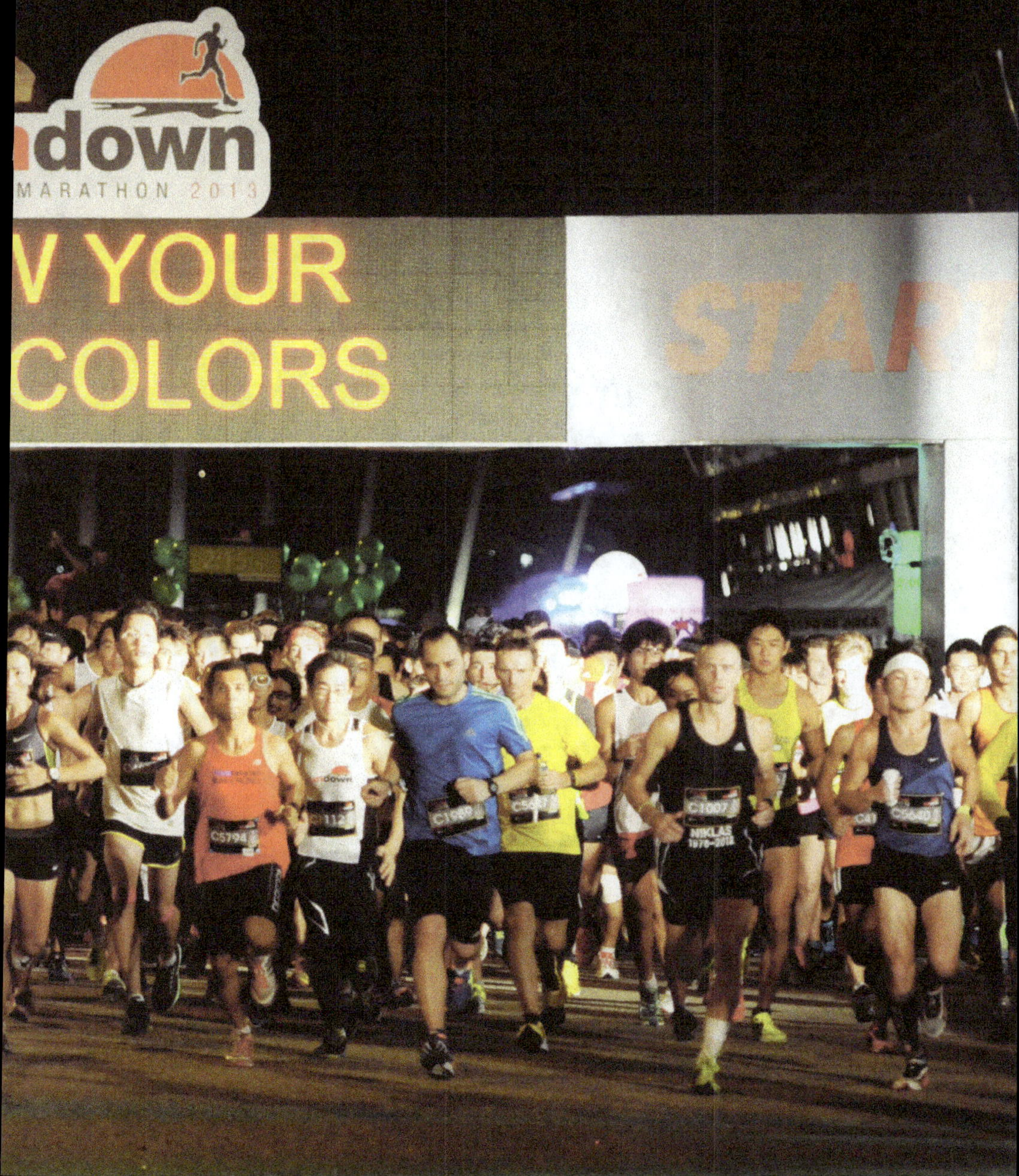

The Experimental Runner

Andy Neo
Sundown Ultra Marathon 2013 — Team relay, 2nd mixed

What is the best way to get Andy Neo talking? Ask about the science of running, how to train effectively, how to avoid injury, and what shoes you should wear. The Sports Marketing Assistant Manager for ASICS Asia is a wealth of information about the sport, having spent many years specialising in sports science — both in his studies and in his career.

But what makes him really special is that he practises everything he preaches — on himself. After completing his national service, he had joined a local running club to stay fit, but found himself lagging behind "all the female and older runners", even though he had been running regularly as an infantry commander in the army. Determined to catch up, he decided to train properly.

"I was doing my degree in sports science and sports education then. So I thought, why not apply some of the training techniques and concepts using myself as a sample?" he says.

In effect, he began experimenting on himself, testing everything he learnt in class on his own body. That approach seemed to work — and would become something he would apply to the rest of his running career. Soon, he found himself able to keep up with the other runners, and even overtake them.

Graduating from Monash University, Australia, with a degree in sports and outdoor education in 2008, he decided to put all his lessons to the ultimate test: He signed up for his first marathon.

It was, in his own words, "really bad". While he clocked a decent five hours, he suffered several injuries, including iliotibial band syndrome (a strain of a ligament running from the thigh down to the shin, often called ITB) and plantar fasciitis, which affects the sole of the feet.

The setback almost made him want to give up running altogether. "But," he adds, "I decided to be a bit more smart in my training. I decided to coach myself."

That set him off on a structured programme that he has been following since 2008. It took much time, commitment and discipline — three to four years — but produced amazing results. He began finishing in the top 10 in the local men's categories in local marathons, and in 2014, clocked his first sub-three hour timing — 2 hrs 57 mins — at the Tokyo Marathon.

Initially, he toyed with the idea of retiring from running altogether, having achieved his long-held target. "I was always telling myself, once I break the three-hour barrier, that's enough, close shop, no more marathons," he says. "Marathons are not easy at all. There's so much suffering, so much commitment, so much sacrifices. Day after day you wake up early just to clock the mileage, and most of the time you train alone."

Runnerdotes

But, he adds, "it's a love and hate relationship. So even though I told myself I don't want to run any more, a few weeks later I started getting itchy."

The following year, he raced at the Tokyo Marathon again, and managed to cut six minutes from his previous timing. "I told myself, 'Wah, if I can go from 2.57 to 2.51, perhaps there's a possibility for me to cut even more, maybe a sub-2.50'," he says. That is his current goal — to break 2 hrs 50 mins before he turns 40, and hopefully even represent Singapore in the Master's Category.

In the meantime, he continues to train — not hard, but "smart".

"A lot of runners make the mistake of really pushing hard during training," he explains. "So come race day, they are not able to peak. There's a peaking window — when you peak too soon, you won't be able to perform your best on race day."

Another problem, he adds, is that runners tend to be impatient. "We want to see results overnight," he says. "But the marathon is a long distance, you need to respect it. You need to be really systematic in your training programme and know exactly what you want."

For Andy, that is building a foundation of strength, which he believes is one of the most important elements for a marathon. What slows a runner down as the miles pass, he explains, is not a lack of speed, but fatigue. "The ability to delay the onset of fatigue gives you a higher chance of a breakthrough," he says.

That means runners need to build strength, so that they can sustain their pace over 42.195 km. This involves two elements — aerobic enhancement, which has to do with the body's production and use of energy; and neuromuscular strength, which is about strength in the muscles.

Andy shares some tips about building strength and other ways to improve your running:

1. Rack up the miles

There are generally two ways for runners to improve their strength, says Andy. One is volume, or sheer mileage, and the other is intensity, which means running hard and fast. "For distance runners, you can't run away from volume," he says. "You need volume to enhance your aerobic tank. It's like driving a small 1.3-litre car. If you want to perform better and race well, you need to expand your tank." Racking up the miles, he says, will teach the body to be more efficient in expending energy.

He has another reason for preferring volume over intensity. "Speed kills," he says simply. "If you do too much speed, the chances of injury are very high. But if you raise the volume without increasing intensity, you have less chance of injuring yourself."

How much volume and intensity should a runner do? One rule of thumb is the 80-20 rule, which recommends runners to have 80 percent of their training focused on aerobic training, and the other 20 percent on speed. As for the optimum level of volume, this will depend on individual runners' ability, he says. "The rule of thumb is that you increase your volume by 10 to 20 percent every block. When you do it that way, you minimise your chances of injury or overtraining."

2. Run up hills

Hill running is an excellent way of building strength, he says. "It's the best gym that a marathon runner can have." By running the same pace on a gradient as that on flat ground, a runner works against gravity and builds neuromuscular strength. It is an efficient way to build strength without

Runnerdotes

going faster. "The mantra is, 'Run slow to run fast'," he says. "You don't really need to run a 4.30 pace in training to run that pace in a marathon."

3. Run in the pool

Aqua running can help build core strength while placing less stress on the joints. Because the water partially supports the runner's weight, running in the pool allows him to strengthen the muscles around his joints (such as the knee), which improves their ability to absorb more of the impact of running on the ground. "Every time you hit the ground, the muscles and soft tissue absorb the impact. But when your muscles start to fatigue, the impact will go to your bones and joints," he explains. "That's why people develop injuries."

There is another advantage of aqua running, he adds. "When you run inside the pool, there is something called hydrostatic pressure, which increases your blood flow and lowers your heart rate."

He recommends running in deep water to work on the big muscles like the glute max, quad and hamstring, and in shallow water to work on the lower extremities, like the ankle and lower calf.

4. Experiment with shoes

As a shoe specialist who has completed the National Shoe Fit Certification Program Level 1, Andy keeps up with the latest trends and technology in running shoes. Amid the ongoing debate on barefoot running, minimalist shoes, maximalist shoes, and traditional cushioned shoes, he takes a nuanced approach.

"As a runner and a self-coach, I believe in mixing all kinds of shoes," he says. "If you always stick to one kind of shoes, your body will adapt to it and no longer be versatile. I do 120 km to 140 km a week, so there's a lot of stress. If I use minimalist shoes, for instance, for 140 km a week for

24 weeks, the chances of my body breaking down and getting injured are high because it is always running in a particular style; there's no variety to it. But if you mix different types of shoes, you give certain muscles a chance to rest while other parts work harder."

5. Run on different terrain

No matter what shoe you wear, Andy stresses, there is something that tends to stay constant: the terrain. In urban Singapore, most runners are pounding the pavement, which subjects their joints to much impact. "You cannot just look at footwear," he says, "you also need to look at the environment you're running in. Even if I give you million-dollar high-tech shoes, it's not going to minimise injuries because the terrain you're running on is not conducive."

He advises running on different types of surfaces, so that the body will adapt to different terrain and use different muscles. That means hitting the undulating trails around MacRitchie Reservoir or the rocky gravel surface around Bedok Reservoir, for instance.

Roads in Singapore are often cambered at an angle to aid water drainage, he adds, and this means runners are actually running at an angle; one side of their bodies is lower than the other. The same thing happens when they run round a track. His solution is to run in both directions, so that it evens out. "Of course," he quickly adds, "you need to consider other users."

6. Bend your knees

The debate over the best type of shoe to wear runs parallel to another debate on the best way to run — heel, midfoot or forefoot striking. Experts and runners alike are divided over which part of the foot should hit the ground first, which is believed to affect the way the body absorbs

 *Runnerdotes*

the shock, as well as speed and efficiency. Again, Andy keeps an open mind. "It's just too naïve to talk about this without considering the many other factors such as hip joints and knee joints," he says. "My advice is to take a step back and look at the entire package holistically."

While many believe that landing with the heel first increases the impact on the knee, Andy notes that many good runners are heel strikers — and do just fine. But he also adds: "The only problem is when you overstride, you tend to lock your knee, and there's a lot of braking force." Straightening the knees when you take a large stride, he explains, means that the legs no longer work like a spring and absorbs the shock of each footfall; the shock is then transferred to other parts of the legs, causing injuries. Instead, runners should aim to have their feet land below their hips if possible, or just in front of their centre of mass, which will help keep their knees bent. "It doesn't matter whether you're a forefoot or midfoot or heel striker," he says, "as long as you bend your knees."

This is especially important when running downhill, when runners are more likely to lengthen their stride and lock their knees when they land. Watch how trail runners come down a slope, he says, and you'll see them zig-zagging down. "They don't come down straight, they tackle it zig-zag, which distributes the load into a lateral mode — left, right, left, right — lessening the impact on their knees."

7. Experiment and experiment

While it is good to listen to the advice of experienced runners, self-coached Andy is big on experimentation. Test it out and see if it works for you, he advises, and don't be afraid to throw it out if it doesn't. "Everyone is unique," he says, "there's no one formula that works for all. You need to find out what are the training methods that work for you, and what are those that don't. If something works for you, just stick with it and try to improve it."

8. Add variety — make it fun

Andy is as big on variety as he is on experimentation. Mix up the shoes, the terrain, the training programme, and even the sports, he says, so that your body remains versatile, flexible and ready to adapt. Apart from running, he enjoys a variety of outdoor sports, including kayaking, mountain trekking, rock climbing and mountain biking.

"If you run the same route, wear the same shoes and hit the same terrain, it will get very monotonous," he says. "You need to inject variety into your programme, make it more fun, more exciting. See everything as a package."

Charging down the hill in the ASICS Beat the Sun event in 2015.

Taking a breather after a hard workout.

Favourite workout: Hill training!

" Marathon is a love and hate relationship. So even though I told myself I don't want to run any more, a few weeks later I started getting itchy. The marathon is a long distance, you need to respect it. You need to be really systematic in your training programme and know exactly what you want. "

Andy Neo

The Road to Rio

Neo Jie Shi
2013 Sundown Marathon — Women's Open 3rd

In a world where elite runners rely heavily on personal coaches, professionally-managed structured training, and detailed nutrition and medical support, Neo Jie Shi achieved an amazing feat: Qualifying for the 2016 Rio Summer Olympics, all on her own.

All the training that the 31-year-old human resources and administration manager had was several years' experience in local races and running with a local running club. Yet she managed to cut down her marathon timing from over five hours to just over three hours, making her one of the fastest runners in Singapore — and putting her onto the road to Rio.

Jie Shi herself would never have imagined representing the Lion City at the Olympics — the first for a Singapore marathoner since Yvonne Danson donned the nation's crescent and stars in 1996. At the Standard

Chartered Marathon Singapore in December 2015, she thought little of it when she finished with a time of 3 hrs 15 mins 6 secs. Though it was a good run, it was more than 30 minutes off the 2016 Rio Olympics' entry standard of 2 hrs 45 mins.

But top marathoner Mok Ying Ren, who was himself trying for Rio, told Jie Shi the stunning news: By finishing in the top 10 at the race — an International Association of Athletics Federations' Gold Label Marathon — Jie Shi had automatically qualified for Rio.

At the time, she recalls, it seemed too good to be true. So she did not quite believe what she was told or place her hopes too high until she received official confirmation the following month. And even then, she still did not dare call herself an Olympian.

"It still feels very surreal to me right now," she says. "I think I was very lucky. To come in 10th in a gold label race in a qualifying year — it was too good to be true. I didn't dare to believe it. I didn't even think too much about it."

After all, she had never considered herself anything more than a "recreational runner".

In junior college, her passion lay in the basketball court, not the road. Towards the end of the first year, her senior encouraged her to join the cross-country running team to make up the numbers for an inter-school competition. She agreed, thinking it would improve her fitness and stamina on the court.

That was when she discovered the joy of running, especially around the Jurong Lake Park, which gave her stunning views of the sunset.

So, when she went on to university, she continued to run regularly around her campus with her friends. One day, a friend suggested signing up for a half-marathon to give themselves a goal to aim for. Jie Shi agreed — and clocked a very creditable sub-2 hours. It was an impressive timing,

 *Runnerdotes*

considering her training had consisted of little more than running around her university campus.

"That's the longest I ever ran!" she says. "But the result motivated me to sign up for the full marathon the following year."

At her first marathon, she managed 5 hrs 20 mins. But within a year, she was whittling it down to 4 hrs 45 mins, then 4 hrs 20 mins. In 2010, bolstered by her improving performance, she joined the Jurong Safra Running Club. Learning to train in a more structured manner, with tempo runs and long runs, soon cut down her timing to 4 hrs 3 mins. It was also there that she would meet her future husband, Jackie Ho.

Jackie, who was then training with the Mount Faber Running Club, introduced Jie Shi to interval training. Soon, she was running four times a week. The training produced results immediately: At the Sundown Marathon in 2011, Jie Shi broke four hours for the first time, coming in eighth in the women's category — her first top 10 finish in a marathon.

It was in 2012, however, that she really made the local marathon scene sit up and take notice. At the Standard Chartered Singapore Marathon, she came in second in the local category. Over the next few years, she would keep taking podium positions at the marathon and other local races.

One of her most memorable races, she says, was the Sundown Marathon in 2013, when she came in third at 3 hrs 30 mins 40 secs.

She had a strong start, staying in the fourth position until the 40 km mark, when she managed to catch up with the runner ahead of her. She overtook the woman, which put her in third place. "For the first time, I had a cyclist riding beside me as I ran," she recalls. "It was one of the most exciting races I ever competed in."

Surging ahead with confidence, she then spotted the next female runner ahead, and started to give chase. For the last 2 km, Jie Shi poured on the fuel, but did not manage to overtake the runner. She came in third in the Women's Open, just seconds behind the woman she had been chasing — fellow Singaporean Ong Kaifen.

"Though I did not manage to catch up with her, I was very happy that I gave my all and earned a surprise third position in the end," she says. "The best part was making a new friend, Kaifen. We have since signed up for a few races together."

That year also gave Jie Shi other races to remember. One was the Boston Marathon in April, which made the headlines when a terrorist attack near the finish line killed several bystanders and injured more than 200 people. Jie Shi, who was running the iconic race for the first time, had passed the finish line — clocking a personal best (PB) of 3 hrs 17 mins 9 secs — not long before.

"The bomb went off after I crossed the finish line and was waiting for my friends. We didn't know what happened; we saw police cars and ambulances. We had heard the explosion but thought it was a gas pipe bursting. It was a tragedy," she says.

A third marathon, in Singapore, also proved to be memorable — albeit for the wrong reason. "I was too ambitious," she says. "I started too fast, so by the time I reached the 35 km mark, I was cramping up so badly that I had to walk and jog. I slipped from third position to sixth in the last 5 km. That reminded me that a marathon is a tough race — you have to respect the distance. Train for it, pace yourself."

The lesson was a valuable one, and was something that would serve her well in subsequent races. "When I first started running, I would go too fast and end up with cramps. So now I'm more careful. If I'm too far from the race pace, I won't get too anxious, because I know I will gradually fall into pace."

She usually aims for an even split, keeping to an even speed that

Runnerdotes

leaves her strength to keep pushing the pace to the end. It was also crucial to her running 3 hrs 15 mins in 2015, which qualified her for Rio. After her entry was confirmed, she was introduced to something new — a personal coach. In early 2016, the Singapore Athletics Association appointed veteran trainer Steven Quek to the self-taught runner, who immediately saw the benefits.

Steven started her on faster interval training and tempo runs, along with a targeted strategy to improve her 10 km timing first, then her half-marathon. Within months, Jie Shi was hitting new highs in her races — a PB of under 40 minutes for 10 km, then a PB of 1 hr 27 mins 39 secs for the half-marathon. With the achievements coming as a real confidence booster, she then began to throw in longer runs and more intensive intervals, and also trained with Steven's students along West Coast Park. On weekends, she joined her own friends to do her long runs.

When she first learnt about the Rio qualification, she toyed with the idea of taking time off or unpaid leave to train full-time. She discussed this idea with her coach, but after studying her training log over the past two years, Steven — who understood how Singapore athletes have to balance family, work and running — advised her to continue working.

"A lot of people told me I should train full-time," she says. "But for me it may not have worked out. Unlike some athletes who have two or three training sessions a day, I was doing only one session. Coach felt that I should continue to do what I had been doing, since it was working out well. The period was too short to make any drastic changes to my training regime; if I suddenly started training two sessions each day, I could end up getting injured. He said what I needed was more rest and recovery."

So Jie Shi kept her daily routine but took time off when needed. "My employer was quite supportive," she says, "he gave me time off on

Tuesday mornings to go for my physiotherapy and weekly massages. That helped a lot."

Finally, the day arrived. August 14, 2016, Sambadrome, Rio de Janeiro. Jie Shi and other Olympic teammates had arrived about two weeks earlier so that they could acclimatise to the time, weather and environment. But as she walked to the start line with 156 other athletes, nothing could prepare her for the excitement and tension. And the heat. Unlike most long-distance races in Singapore, which start around dawn or even before, the Rio marathon was scheduled to start at 9.30 am.

"Many of us were pouring mineral water over our heads," she recalls. "Then the race just started pretty suddenly. Everyone was cheering. But I stayed at the back — I couldn't really squeeze to the front, and I know my own ability."

Indeed, she knew she had to be realistic. Her own PB of 3 hrs 9 mins 57 secs was about 20 minutes slower than the Olympic qualifying time, and four years ago in London, the women's champion had clocked an Olympic record of 2 hrs 23 mins 7 secs. The Singaporean was even prepared to be the last one across the finish line.

So when she found herself at the end of the pack with another runner, Saudi Arabia's Attar Sarah, she stayed cool and kept to her targeted pace. "I tried to remain focused," she says. "We were running together for a while. Then, after about 2 km, I thought I should run a bit faster to get my target pace, so I ran a bit ahead. I was the second-last runner then."

About 18 km later, Jie Shi managed to catch up with Cambodia's Ly Nary. The route included three loops of 10 km, so she could see the faster runners going past her in the opposite direction on the other side of the road. "I could see all the elite runners. In a way, I was a spectator — I got to see them run — while I myself was participating in the race," she says.

 *Runnerdotes*

By this time, all the other runners were also starting to find that the biggest challenge came not just from the competition, but also from the Brazilian heat. "When we started, it wasn't too high, about 18 to 20 degrees Celsius," says Jie Shi. But when we reached midday, it was really hot. I knew I couldn't sustain my pace. I just kept pouring water over myself, trying not to think about the weather."

What kept her going, she says, was the support of spectators — including those from other countries. "The spectators were all carrying different flags. But when they saw me coming, they recognised the flag on my vest and cheered me on, 'Singapore! Singapore! Singapore!'" she recalls. "That was very heart-warming and it motivated me to keep pressing on and try to close up the gap with the person in front."

As she slowly narrowed the gap between her and the scattered runners in front, the Saudi Arabian runner caught up with her around the 32 km mark, then overtook her. Jie Shi responded, and tried to keep Attar Sarah in sight. Soon, the two women were running together as they completed the third and last 10 km loop.

"It felt like we both wanted the company, so that we would not be lonely," she says with a chuckle. "Sarah was still ahead of me when we headed into the Porto Maravilha region. I managed to overtake her as we ran past the Museum of Tomorrow, at around 37 km. Then I just kept going until the finish line. The last 500 m was the longest 500 m I ever ran. By then, I was struggling and hoping that I wouldn't get cramps. I was so glad to finish it."

Jie Shi came in 131st out of 133 finishers, with a time of 3 hrs 15 mins 18 secs. It was a most remarkable performance, given that 23 runners did not complete the race.

The Singaporean runner will never forget running at the Olympics. But her takeaways from the experience go far beyond simply running at

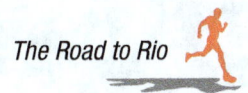
The Road to Rio

one of the biggest races in the world. It was about moulding her into a better person.

"Running has made me a more confident person," she says. "It has taught me about overcoming challenges and adversity. Sometimes, when life gets too busy, I literally run away to relieve stress. After running, I'll come back to my work and see that with any problems in life, you can find a solution. Running gives me balance in life. It's a happy pill."

At the famed Boston Marathon finish line in 2013.

With my coach Steven Quek at the Rio Olympics' opening ceremony. A great honour to represent Singapore at the Olympics, joining the ranks of previous greats who had flown the flag proudly before me.

Giving all I have for a local PB finish at the Standard Chartered Marathon Singapore 2015.

Happy and humbled to run alongside world class marathoners and successfully completed the Rio Olympics marathon 2016.

" Running has made me a more confident person and taught me about overcoming adversity. Running a marathon can be quite challenging and I know if I can overcome this challenge, I can overcome any challenges that come along in work or in life. Sometimes when life gets too busy, I literally run away to relieve stress. I always feel better after a run. Running may not solve all my problems but it certainly helps me to see things from another perspective and make better decisions in work and in life. Running keeps me balance in life. It's my happy pill. "

Neo Jie Shi

Going for Gold

Soh Rui Yong
Ambassador for OSIM Sundown Marathon 2016

It was a hard battle fought over 42.195 km, but in the end, Soh Rui Yong's race to a gold medal came down to the last 400 m. And that's when he found that patience always pays off, especially when you're in the race of your life.

It was June 7, 2015, and Rui Yong had been keeping pace with the race leaders in the South-east Asian (SEA) Games marathon over the better part of two hours in Singapore. One by one, however, they slipped back, leaving the Singaporean and Thai rival Boonthung Srisung at the front. Neck and neck, the duo passed the 30 km mark, then 35 km, 40 km, 41 km… and still, neither man made the move to surge ahead.

Both runners knew that the final "kick", or sprint, had to be timed exactly right: too early or too late, and the race was lost. Boonthung had very good finishing speed, and Rui Yong knew that he had to bide his time. If he took off too early, the Thai runner might be able to overtake him in the home stretch. So, he patiently kept to the Thai's heels.

Then the bell went, signifying the last lap. It was now or never.

Ask Rui Yong if he had ever imagined himself in this scene, and he would probably laugh. When he was 10 years old, he says, he had trouble keeping up with his mum, an avid jogger. "She liked to go for 3 km, 5 km runs around the neighbourhood, and would drag me along. But I hated it! I was always stopping. I wasn't naturally fit."

The next year, however, he took part in school sports day, and to his surprise, came in first in the long jump as well as 800 m race, second in the 200 m, and third in the 100 m. The next year, he won the 1,500 m, and was fielded at the national schools competition, where he finished eighth at the same race. "That's when I figured out this was something I could be reasonably good at," he says.

In secondary school, he was drafted into the cross-country team. "I don't think I was ever super serious about running," he admits. "But I would go for training and put in my best effort because I didn't want to lose to anyone. I would do everything right — make sure I warmed up properly, do my drills — not because I was super disciplined, but because I wanted to beat everyone. The competitive spirit that kept me going."

He was partly inspired by what he saw happening at local races. Runs like the Sundown Marathon were drawing people from all walks of life, and many came not to win, but just to be part of the fun. One day, he thought to himself, I will figure out why they enjoy it so much.

That day came not long after. After coming under the tutelage of veteran distance running coach Steven Quek, Rui Yong not only began to take running seriously, but also learn to enjoy it. "He was a great mentor," he says. "He really helped me conduct myself in a professional manner. He made such a big impact on my life."

 *Runnerdotes*

Another turning point came when Rui Yong qualified for the Asean Schools Games in 2009. At the Games in Suphanburi, Thailand, he won gold in the 3000 m steeplechase. "Representing Singapore was kind of cool," he says. "It was a privilege and honour, and I wanted to do it at a larger scale. The SEA Games became a dream for me."

That dream drove him to train hard after he finished national service — and it saw results. Rui Yong managed to cut his 5 km timing down to 15 mins 36 secs, his 10 km timing to 32 mins 26 secs, and his half-marathon timing down to 1 hr 12 mins 12 secs. "Everything was going really well," he says.

In August 2013, he went to Oregon, US, to study, and it was there that he found a new burst of speed. Training in what he calls the "running capital" of America, he found great inspiration watching top runners at work. "I soaked up whatever the elites were doing," he recalls. "It was so eye-opening. I was running 50 km to 60 km a week in Singapore and people thought I was crazy. In Oregon, people were running 160 km a week. I realised that's what it takes to be running at that high level."

Increasing his mileage and picking up tips, he found his timings dropping even more. He cut his half-marathon timing to 1 hr 10 mins 28 secs, and soon, was breaking his personal bests (PB) for the 5 km, 10 km, and half-marathon. In 2014, he broke the Singapore 10 km record — set by P.C. Suppiah in 1973 — at a track and field meet, with 31 mins 15 secs. His 5 km timing dropped to 15 mins 8 secs, and half-marathon, to 1 hr 7 mins 52 secs.

Then, at the California International Marathon in December 2014, he really made Singapore sit up. It was his debut marathon, but the 23-year-old clocked a jaw-dropping 2 hrs 26 mins 1 sec. To put it in perspective, it was even faster than the SEA Games qualifying mark of 2 hrs 30 mins set by Singapore Athletics, and 29 seconds faster than the personal best of the No. 1 Singaporean marathoner at the time, Mok Ying Ren.

That amazing performance not only put him on the radar, but also qualified him for the SEA Games the following year. Rui Yong's dream had come true.

It meant, however, that he really had to step up his training. This saw him ramping up his mileage and even taking an extended time off studies to go for high-altitude training in Flagstaff, Arizona. The exposure to thin, dry air, challenging trails and Olympic-level runners showed results: On returning to Oregon, he set a new personal best of 14 mins 58 secs for 5 km, in the middle of a marathon training cycle.

Flying back to Singapore several weeks ahead of the SEA Games, however, he found himself struggling to acclimatise to the time difference, heat and humidity.

"I was just so jet-lagged and tired," he recalls. "After workouts, I would be lying on the ground wondering whether I could adjust in time." But he found inspiration — and some stress — from passers-by who recognised him and encouraged him. "It started to hit me how much people were looking to me to win this for Singapore," he says.

That, and an improving performance, led to a confident Rui Yong on race day. He calls it a "weird confidence" that grew in the last week leading to the Games and which he still cannot quite explain. "Maybe your words and actions can communicate with your mind," he says. "I was putting on a bit of a game — I would talk big and keep saying, 'I'm going to win.' My dad commented that I sounded like a boxer or sprinter, not a marathon runner!"

Just before the race, he recalls, he was asked by then Minister for Culture, Community and Youth Lawrence Wong and Singapore Athletics president Tang Weng Fei about his chances against the race favourite,

Runnerdotes

Philippine SEA Games gold medallist Eduardo Buenavista. To which Rui Yong replied, "Eduardo is a really good runner, he's won 10 gold medals. If I was a betting man, I would put my money on him… to win the silver medal, because I'm going to win the gold."

"Everyone started laughing," he chuckled. "But I was thinking to myself, 'If you don't win now, you're really going to look like an idiot!' I don't know why I said that. For some reason, I felt that talking it up boosted my confidence and bluffed myself into thinking I was better than I actually was."

Still, he did not let his confidence interfere with his strategy — one of patience. This was to pace himself and "not do anything dumb" for the first 30 km or so, and rely on his stamina and speed for a surge at the end. So when the gun went off, he started slowly, keeping pace with the leaders but not making any big moves.

At around 6 km, the race took an unexpected turn when race marshals misdirected some of the runners, which resulted in them having to do a U-turn to get back on course. This upset the order and Rui Yong suddenly found himself at the rear.

"People who were behind me were now in front," he says. "But I thought, don't get mad over something like that, you can't control it. Just get back into the game slowly."

So, patiently, he worked his way forward again, catching up with fellow Singaporean Ashley Liew. Ashley had run the right route and had now ended up at the front of the pack. When Ashley appeared keen to speed up when passed, Rui Yong told him, "Just tuck in behind them, let's wait it out."

Keeping to his strategy of patience, Rui Yong kept his cool even when Boonthung and Eduardo sped up, which left the rest of the runners trailing by as much as 40 seconds at one point. Rui Yong resisted the temptation to sprint ahead to catch up.

"I just ran a super patient race," he says. "At some point, they were 200 m ahead and I couldn't see them. But I thought, 'This is a marathon, in the grand scheme of things 45 seconds is not really a big margin'."

Eventually, however, Rui Yong and Vietnam's Nguyen Thanh Hoang slowly caught up with the two in front, but again, just hung on behind them, careful not to tire himself out by pushing the pace.

Soon, Eduardo dropped back, and Rui Yong found himself just behind Boonthung, who seemed content to take a relatively easy pace. The Thai runner, he could see, was playing a "tactical game". This was a first for Rui Yong, but he figured that he had to "think" through the race and respond to the other runners, rather than just run his own race. So he played it cool.

"I knew he was pretty fast finisher," he says. "I could see that he was trying to keep it slow right to the end, then use his speed to outkick us. So I said, 'I'm just going to wait'."

This went on for kilometre after kilometre, until Boonthung picked up a pace a little at 30 km, leaving Nguyen behind. Rui Yong kept pace, staying with him for another 10 km. By this time, all the runners' clothes and shoes were soaking wet from a thunderstorm, and they were running with strong winds that either pushed them forward or pulled them back.

Then, the two men pulled into Kallang Practice Track for the final stretch, Rui Yong just a whisker behind the Thai. The 42.195 km race was coming down to the last few hundred metres. "This is going to be the biggest 400 m of your life," Rui Yong remembers telling himself. "It all comes down to this — win or lose, there's nothing in between. As I stepped into the stadium, I could hear everyone screaming and shouting. I had some flashbacks going through my head, but I woke up and thought, 'Okay, stop dreaming, you still have a race to run'."

 *Runnerdotes*

When the bell went, Boonthung still did not appear to want to make the final kick. The 400 m mark passed, then 300 m, and still no move from the Thai runner. As they approached the 200 m point, Rui Yong drew even. Then he decided to go for it.

"I gave him a look, then I went off hard," he says of those final moments. "It was the most scary race I had ever run in my life. I didn't look back, I just went as hard as I could. Everyone was screaming and shouting because he was right on my shoulder. With 100 m to go, I couldn't take it, so I sneaked a look, and saw him some distance behind. That's when I knew I had it."

Raised both arms triumphantly, Rui Yong crossed the finish line in 2 hrs 34 mins 56 secs. Boonthung came in just 13 seconds later.

"It was a memorable day, a memorable experience," says Rui Yong. "Winning a marathon for your country on home soil is bigger than anything I will ever do."

The victory validated his strategy of patience. By not rushing the pace, he had kept enough reserve for his last burst. It also confirmed what he had learnt from experience — that the halfway point of a 42 km race was not 21 km, but 32 km, when a runner's body runs down its glycogen stores. That can make the last 10 km feel as long as the first 32 km, he says.

"Don't make any huge moves till the 32 km mark, because it is too early to tell if your body is in its best shape," he advises. "You can never start off too slow."

Within months, however, he was to find his patience tested again.

With a SEA Games gold medal in the bag, he now felt he had a realistic shot at another big prize — a place at the Rio Olympics the following year. Rui Yong's PB of 2 hrs 26 mins was just seven minutes off the Olympic qualifying standard of 2 hrs 19 mins, and he felt he had a pretty good chance if he put in enough training. If he made it, he would be the first Singaporean to qualify for an Olympic marathon.

"It wasn't easy," he acknowledges, "but it wasn't undoable. If you don't have a goal that excites you, then it's not a goal worth having."

But as Rui Yong tried to squeeze in more training while wrapping up his studies in Oregon, he was struck by the very thing all runners fear: Injury. Trying to balance schoolwork and 160 km of mileage a week with insufficient rest resulted in plantar fasciitis. A common injury among runners, the inflammation of tissue on the sole of the feet makes every footstep painful and can take weeks or even months to heal.

He did all he could to address the injury, resorting to painkillers at one point, but it did not heal in time. He pulled out of one race, then mustered only 2 hrs 37 mins 33 secs at the London Marathon in April 2016, well short of the Olympic qualifying time. The Gold Coast Marathon in Australia in June was his last chance, but by that time he knew that the only sensible option was not to aggravate the injury any further. The road to Rio was closed.

Once again, he had to play the game of patience, and give his foot time to heal. And once again, he saw results. At the Chicago Marathon in October, he beat his own PB, coming in at 2 hrs 24 mins 55 secs.

"That was a big result for me," he says, "because no matter how confident you are, there's always that nagging thought that once you lose your mojo, you can't get it back. After being injured, I kept thinking, 'Am I really done? Is this foot never going to allow me to race the same way any more?' In Chicago I went off with a very conservative start, but once I caught fire halfway, it felt great to be running my best again."

His latest record also means that he qualifies for the 2017 SEA Games in Kuala Lumpur — and hopefully, another shot at the Tokyo Summer Olympics in 2020.

"Chicago was just the start of a new beginning," he says. "I don't think I'm going to be done anytime soon."

On scoring his Personal Best at the Chicago Marathon 2016:

" That was a big result for me, because no matter how confident you are, there's always that nagging thought that once you lose your mojo, you can't get it back. After being injured, I kept thinking, 'Am I really done? Is this foot never going to allow me to race the same way any more?' In Chicago I went off with a very conservative start, but once I caught fire halfway, it felt great to be running my best again. "

Soh Rui Yong

Just Run

Jeanette Wang
Sundown Ultra Marathon 2007 — Women's champion
Sundown Ultra Marathon 2008 — Women's champion

It was at the halfway point of the race that Jeanette Wang knew she had gone too fast. Some 80 km into an ultramarathon, she found that she was in the top 10. Most people would have been pleased, but Jeanette shook her head realistically. Aware that her competitors were world-class, she realised that she was probably running faster than she should, given her own capability. With another 80 km of steep, winding, rocky trails left to go on Mount Fuji in Japan, she knew she was going to pay the price for her initial speed.

True enough, some 30 km later, Jeanette's first 168 km trail ultramarathon in 2013 came to a shuddering halt.

"I was kind of dying," she recalls. "I was just sprawled on the trail. I had zero energy. I couldn't lift my legs, I couldn't even stand up; there was nothing left in me. I sat on the huge roots of a tree, hung my head and said, 'Okay, I'm going to give up now'."

Pulling out her mobile phone, she messaged a friend in Hong Kong. Keep going, he replied. One step at a time. Finish this 100 miles, then you don't have to do it ever again. Then, fellow competitors whom she knew ran past and shouted words of encouragement. "C'mon, c'mon!" they yelled. "Let's go!"

Jeanette took another look around her and realised that even if she gave up now, she would still have to find her way out of the wilderness. "Look," she told herself, "you've come all the way here, you've put in the training, you've put in the money. Think about the nice holiday you're going to have after that. Oh, come on, Jeanette, just get on with it."

And she did. Somehow, she found the strength to stand up, then to move forward step by step, using her hands to lift each leg in turn. For the next two, three hours, she shuffled forward. Then, as the food and water she downed in an effort to pump energy back into her tired body started to take effect, she found herself starting to run again. "It was like getting a new life in a computer game — ding, ding, ding, you can go again!" she recalls. "Soon I was fine and running, and I ran strong to the finish."

Jeanette finished 17th overall. It would not have been possible, she says, if she had not forced herself to get through what she calls the "tough moments". "Every race has its tough moments," she explains. "There are very few races where I've felt good all the way. You just need to grind through them and remind yourself that there's light at the end of the tunnel."

And, she stresses, there's no secret nor shortcut. "Getting through tough moments is really all in the mind. To train the mind, you just have to go out and run and race more. The more tough moments you experience, the better you get at handling them. I don't know of any other way."

 *Runnerdotes*

It is a lesson that Jeanette learnt through a long journey — literally.

Jeanette's exposure to running started relatively early. In primary and secondary school, she played netball competitively. Her fitness drew the attention of her teacher, who recruited her to the cross-country as well as track and field teams, which saw her excelling especially in the longer distances. In junior college, she was inspired by the "cool triathlon T-shirts" worn by a physical education teacher — Leong Chee Mun, who was in Singapore's first Everest team — to try out longer runs, which eventually culminated in marathons as well as triathlons.

Over the next 10 years or so, Jeanette would rack up successes in numerous local and regional races. From biathlons and duathlons to aquathlons and triathlons, she kept taking podium positions, or coming in top 10 or top 20 even when competing against world-class triathletes in her age group.

One of her proudest moments was coming in 13th in her age category at the Ironman World Championship in Kona, Hawaii — widely seen as the Holy Grail of Ironman events — in 2006. She also set a national record of 12 hrs 9 mins 38 secs. (The record was later broken by Choo Ling Er.)

Then, Jeanette began to tire of triathlons. "I felt that I did all the iconic races that I had to do in the sport," she says. Her busy schedule as a journalist didn't help, as it made it increasingly difficult to keep up the training. It was then that she discovered a new challenge: ultramarathons.

Taking runners well beyond the standard marathon distance of 42.195 km, these long races typically cover 50 km, 100 km, 100 miles or even more, and can push runners to the very limits. They not only require high levels of physical endurance, but also demand nothing less than total mental commitment. Many ultramarathons also involve trail running, adding an extra dose of difficulty.

While Jeanette's fitness and endurance, gained from years of triathlons, stood her in good stead for ultramarathons, she found that these races extracted even more from runners.

"In an Ironman, you use different muscles for the different disciplines, from swimming to cycling to running. You also don't have to carry your energy gels or drinks, because there are aid stations along the way. In an ultra, you just batter your legs all the time. And you have to carry your own things," she says.

So, when Jeanette signed up for the Sundown Ultramarathon in 2008, she knew that she had to give it total commitment, as she had never covered 84 km on her feet before.

"There is no secret to doing well in an ultra," she says. "You have to put in the training. I had a proper training plan that built up mileage from short to long runs, up to six hours. I would do it before work — start at 3.30 am or 4 am, then cheekily turn up a bit late for work. There's no secret at all."

She also mixed the long runs with speed work — repetitions of short but fast runs — and rest. This, she stresses, was absolutely essential. "A lot of people find it difficult to rest. They think you're lazy when you don't train. But resting, or active recovery, is actually a key to keeping you fresh."

The strategy paid off. At the inaugural Sundown Ultramarathon in 2008, Jeanette became the first woman to break the tape, coming in at 9 hrs 14 mins 36 secs. Not only that, she went on defend her title the next year, with an even better time of 8 hrs 47 mins 36 secs.

Jeanette, however, is quick to add that she was "lucky". At the third edition of the Sundown Ultramarathon in 2010, where she dropped out after about 50 km, the women's top spot was taken by Anne Hui Qi with a time of 8 hrs 4 secs. "Her time was absolutely phenomenal," exclaims

 *Runnerdotes*

Jeanette. "There was no way I could have matched her. So I was lucky to win the first two years — I was at the right place at the right time, taking part in the right race."

But while the double Sundown victories were a culmination of years of training, as far as Jeanette is concerned, her days of competitiveness are over.

"Having competed since I was in school, I feel like I'm actually tired of competing," she admits. These days, she just wants to "experience more".

The sea change in her attitude came after two significant events in her life — moving to Hong Kong in 2011, and the birth of her daughter Marla in 2014. There, she discovered the joy of exploring the many trails outside the city, far from the maddening crowds. Now, she says, her greatest joy comes not from taking home another trophy, but from trying out a new race or route in a new country. (That's how she ended up on Mount Fuji in Japan in 2013, attempting her first 100-miler.)

Her philosophy of running has also changed with the advent of motherhood. While she still loves running, she now sees it through her daughter's eyes. Few things bring Jeanette more joy than exploring the hills ringing Hong Kong with her two-year-old in a baby carrier on her back. This slows the former top triathlete and ultramarathoner down from a race-pace run to a slow hike, which she says has taught her to appreciate the beauty around her, and the wonder of spending time with her daughter.

"Marla enjoys being out there with me," she says. "My daughter inspires me because she reminds me of the carefreeness of youth. She's so happy. If we can just remember the simple things, we would be so much happier."

Jeanette still runs, of course. But instead of having her life revolving

around fixed training sessions, as she used to do, she now fits running around her day. And her "whims and fancies".

"My training now is completely unstructured — no timetable, no training diary. I go by feel," she says. "If I wake up and don't feel like going for a run, I don't go for a run. If I feel like I want to go stair climbing instead of running, I do that. Or if I want to go hiking with my daughter, I do that. It goes hand in hand with me wanting to experience rather than compete."

After years of biathlons, triathlons, marathons, and ultramarathons, she has finally learnt the true joy of running. "Sometimes, when you're so focused on preparing for a race, you can take away the joy," she says.

She even avoids trying to derive lessons about life from running, whether it is about not giving up or taking one step at a time. "I think sometimes we philosophise too much," she observes. "In the end, it's just a simple thing: Just go out and run, and don't think so much. Enjoy the fresh air, the trail, the serenity, the peace, the quiet and the time alone. Do it for your physical and mental health, but don't think so much. Just go out and enjoy."

Me and my greatest running pal, my daughter, Marla. (photo credit: Lloyd Belcher)

Chugging up fully geared at the MSIG Lautau 50 event in 2016.

Rambling downhill fearlessly at the Oakley Trail Half-series in Hong Kong.

" In the end, it's just a simple thing: Just go out and run, and don't think so much. Enjoy the fresh air, the trail, the serenity, the peace, the quiet and the time alone. Do it for your physical and mental health, but don't think so much. Just go out and enjoy. My daughter, Marla enjoys being out there with me. She inspires me because she reminds me of the carefreeness of youth. She's so happy. If we can just remember the simple things, we would be so much happier. "

Jeanette Wang

From Late Bloomer to SEA Games Athlete

Melvin Wong Yao Hian
Sundown Marathon 2016 — Team of 4 relay Male 1st

When Melvin Wong first started doing triathlons in 2006, his primary aim was to overcome his fear of water. Gradually, he developed a love for the sport, and even found himself doing quite well in local and regional races.

What he could not have imagined, however, was that years later, he would represent Singapore, as a runner, in the South-east Asian Games. But that was exactly what happened in 2015, when the 32-year-old found himself lining up alongside top racers in the region at the 5,000 m and 10,000 m finals.

It was an amazing achievement for the self-confessed late bloomer, who had moved from triathlons to running-only races in 2012 after he got married. "To keep up with trying to be a competitive triathlete, and to balance work and family, was quite challenging," he says. "So I just focused on one sport instead of three."

Runnerdotes

Not surprisingly, his experience as a triathlete put him in good stead for middle-distance races of 5 km to 10 km, and he began taking home medals in local and regional races. Encouraged to consider more structured training, Melvin went under the wing of former national runner Elangovan Ganesan in 2014. It turned out to be a fortuitous move.

"I've always viewed myself as an above-average runner, but when it comes to trying to be like the top runner at national level, I didn't think I was doing the right things," he recalls. "But training under Elangovan's guidance opened my eyes to how a structured programme works, and how training with a group can really push you beyond what you think you can do."

Melvin soon discovered how prophetic this thought would turn out to be.

His fellow trainees were setting their eyes on the SEA Games in 2015, but while he was caught up in the excitement, Melvin remained realistic. "At that point I knew I wasn't at that level to compete in the 5,000 m and 10,000 m," he says. "So I didn't have too much expectation, although I did bring it up to my coach, and we agreed that we would take things as they came along."

So, through the end of 2014 and into 2015, he continued training "as usual". But when he joined in some extra sessions that his coach arranged for Raviin Muthu Kumar, who was eyeing the 1,500 m, and Muhammad Shah Feroz, who specialised at the 3,000 m steeplechase, Melvin began to see his own timings improve. That was when he and his coach began to harbour real hope of making the cut for the 5,000 m and 10,000 m races. Not long after, the good news arrived — Melvin was selected to run for Singapore at the Games.

Determined to make a strong showing, and with support from his employer, family and colleagues, he took time off work to train full-time.

This meant hitting the track, gym or road seven days a week to build up his speed, endurance and strength. The exercises, from intervals and tempos to longer-distance runs, pushed him hard. Each week, he would rack up 140 km to 145 km, had to aim for target times with little or no rest between sprints, and kept moving throughout entire sessions. Training for the 10,000 m was especially intense. For example, he had to run 3.2 km at race pace, slow down to an easy jog for a round or two, then speed up for 2.4 km.

"This is crucial because it helps the body to recognise that kind of mental rough patch you have to go through," he explains.

The efforts paid off. In March, he participated in 5,000 m and 10,000 m events at the Singapore Open and Malaysia Open to test his progress. At the 10,000 m, he clocked 33 hrs 40 mins 28 secs, a personal best (PB).

And so it was, on June 9, 2015, that he found himself at the start line in the National Stadium, ready for the 5,000 m. It was a bit "nerve-wrecking", he admits, knowing the kind of mental and physical pain he would have to go through to cover the 12½ laps. And when the gun went off, there was a surprise awaiting him. "I didn't expect the pace to be so hard right from the start," he recalls. "We were spread out within the first few laps."

As the faster runners left Melvin, fellow Singaporean Jeevaneesh Soundararajah and several others behind, it was all Melvin could do to stay focused. "Although it was a short race, a lot of it was more mental than physical," he says. "You're trying to rally yourself to maintain your splits, to close the gap, and to try and do everything just to squeeze that performance out of yourself. It was tough. Although I was focusing on my own race, I was on my own 80 percent of the time, so there was no one in my vicinity to target. Mentally, it was draining."

To avoid getting distracted, he focused on hitting his pre-determined

lap times. "Every 400 m lap I passed, I had an alarm to remind me how far I was off. That helped me to focus on the next round, to see if I could aim closer to my goal. I also broke the track down into four portions of 100 m, which helped me a fair bit. Even though I was in a lot of pain, I tried to think of all these things to help me pull through, to keep my mind from thinking so much."

In the end, he finished a respectable seventh out of 10 runners, clocking 16 mins 1.58 secs. Even though he had had no expectations of bringing back a medal, he admits to feeling a little disappointed, as he had not managed to beat his own PB of 15 mins 46 secs. But he knew he had to remain focused, because in 24 hours' time, he would be back on the track for the second — and harder — race, the 10,000 m.

The next day was one to remember. Encouraged by thousands of cheering fans, Melvin made the headlines with a final burst of speed near the end, powering ahead of his closest rival to come in seventh out of eight. "The last 600 m," he recalls, "was emotional." He crossed the finish line at 32 mins 59.10 secs, smashing his PB of 33 mins 40 secs. While he did not come back with a medal, as far as he was concerned, he had attained his goal.

The achievement taught him several important lessons, one of which was simply this: Believe in yourself. "I came back with the belief that I could do more; I just hadn't shown it yet," he says.

The other was staying focused. "It's easy to get distracted in a race," he explains. "You can get caught up trying to match up with your competitors, but I always find that the most soothing thing for me is to have faith in what you've done in training, and to replicate the same thing on race day. That part gives me the confidence — I know I've done it in training, so I can do it on race day, and I shouldn't be distracted by my peers."

He has since returned to his job and tuned down his training, but he still trains at least four times a week — short intervals on one day, core-related exercises on another, repetitions on a third, and a long run during the weekend. All these workouts come on top of 10-hour days at the office as a Sales Associate and family, which grew when he became a father in August 2016. To balance his many commitments, he plans well ahead, allocating time for work, family and training, and making sure he keeps to schedule.

What keeps him going? Easy question: It's the next Games. He may be realistic about his ability, but it has not stopped him from his dream of getting a medal the next time he steps up to the starting line. "That's something I haven't achieved yet. That means I am not at that level yet; there's room for me to improve," he says.

Looking back, he believes that the 2015 SEA Games, which was held in Singapore for the first time in 22 years, has given athletes like himself a much-needed boost. "This inclusion of more local athletes gives us a bit of hope, a bit of confidence to embark on more."

Victory moment for me after achieving my personal best in 10,000 m at the Southeast Asian Games in 2015.

My biggest fan and supporter – my wife, Saffry.

Hammering out with all I have at the Southeast Asian Games 2015 5,000 m event.

> "It's easy to get distracted in a race. You can get caught up trying to match up with your competitors, but I always find that the most soothing thing for me is to have faith in what you've done in training, and to replicate the same thing on race day. That part gives me the confidence – I know I've done it in training, so I can do it on race day, and I shouldn't be distracted by my peers."

Melvin Wong

Don't Stop Running

Adrian Mok

As I recount the memories of the night runs, I relish every moment of the adventure. Many people think running is monotonous and boring, but I find myself at the most creative when I'm out on a long run. Runs that do not take up intense lung capacity but are conducted at a bearable aerobic pace can be therapeutic. I think through things, problems, strategies, ideas and solutions.

For many people, the fear of running — or, indeed, the rejection of any notion of exercise — comes from the discomfort associated with the exercise. However, once you get past the conditioning phase, you'll find that the body is a pretty amazing machine. It adapts, it grows, it repairs and it recovers. We get stronger with every single step we take. Each moment of every run lays another brick on the foundation of the house.

Through the wonderful conversations I had with all the athletes featured in *Runnerdotes*, I discovered that they don't just love running; they fall in love with it. They are in it head over heels. They pursue it. They sacrifice for it without complaining. They serve their training routines again and again, seeking to build up their bodies to withstand the test of the next race.

I know what that feels like. I can identify with these athletes' passion — as well as their competitive, fiery streak. But their rivalry comes not from other athletes; it comes from themselves. They are their biggest competitor. Try heading out for a run in the rain, for a hard workout, for laps on the track in the wee hours or early morning, and try doing it alone. The power we draw on comes from the drive to better ourselves, to beat the Cannot and the Will Not.

In the world of distance running, "bonking" or "hitting the wall" is a familiar experience. Scientifically, it is explained by the depletion of glycogen (carbohydrate stores) in the body. This causes a dip in the blood sugar level, which triggers the brain to slow down all physical actions as well as mental concentration. Scientifically, the solution to this problem is feeding the body with sugar so that it can then resume its normal functions. The obvious strategy is thus to consume sugary foodstuff, which will replenish one's energy.

But ultramarathoners do the exact opposite: We try not to give in to the temptation to take in food so quickly. The idea is to push the body to draw on its store of fat rather than on its precious store of glycogen, a premium fuel. However, this process means that we have to deal with the problem of "hitting the wall" — and overcoming it. It means developing strategies to overcome these tough moments. (At times, I have slowed down to a walking pace, telling myself that I would eventually feel better.) It takes great mental resilience to use the mind to overcome the hunger pangs.

 *Runnerdotes*

Many see athletes as people who love pain. They think we enjoy punishment and suffering. Really? Do we? In the toughest of moments, I have asked myself this question. And my answer is: No — as a flesh-and-blood human being, I do not enjoy these terrible moments. But we have learnt to develop strategies to embrace these moments. We fight it; we choose not to give in. And as we learn to overcome each of these moments, we get physically stronger and mentally tougher. It is this spirit of stretching our personal limits that gives us the shot of adrenaline. Perhaps we are addicted, but these are the little celebratory milestones that every single training session brings. This is the reason we hone our craft, the reason we get out there and do what we love doing.

The creation of Sundown Marathon came from these moments. I have often wondered if many people share my habit or revelation. Why would anyone want to push his or her body to run through the night? When the notion of a night marathon was first mooted, I thought of giving people an option to run the route twice, but did not expect many lunatics to subscribe to the idea. Much to my surprise, the first edition of Sundown Marathon in 2008 saw more than 600 people attempt the 84 km category. Overall, we saw more than 6,000 runners gathering in a corner of Changi Park, ready to overcome the night.

The journey of Sundown has not been an easy one. Much like the stories of adventures — or misadventures — of my night runs, the Sundown Marathon has had its share of thrills and spills, and has evolved over the years. We have seen the event grow exponentially, and we have struggled to find funds to scale it up and to find a bigger, more suitable venue. We have suffered a backlash over congestion, insufficient hydration supplies, and unlighted routes. We have had tough years when sponsors pulled out of the event. We have split up with business partners over how we should grow the company and expand the race. And we have had to keep the ultramarathon going through several years even when we were losing money.

Coming into our 10th year, I have relished every single defeat. In my darkest moments in running, I have learnt to draw strength and to conceive positivity. These were lessons I applied to the Sundown Marathon business.

My objective is pure and simple: I want to spread the joy of running to as many crazy people out there as I can. I want to find more people who will endorse my attitude of "hard-core" and advocate it to others. In the early years of Sundown, I came up with the theme "Sleep Can Wait" with the idea that "hard-core" need not apply only to serious athletes. Rather it is an attitude that anyone can adopt when they face a challenge. The spirit of Sundown is about pushing oneself to overcome sleep and run through the night. This is a long journey, but we will push our limits, as we do with our physical bodies when we run. I hope runners will find the mental strength as they learn how to cope with adversities in life.

Never stop loving, never stop running.

www.ingramcontent.com/pod-product-compliance
Lightning Source LLC
Chambersburg PA
CBHW061943220426
43662CB00012B/2004